NO DESTINATION

No Destination

Satish Kumar

ST DEINIOL'S LIBRARY

HAWARDEN

Cancelled from
Gladstone's Library

2 4 JUL 2024

GLADSTONE'S
LIBRARY

Mochyn Du/Black Pig Press

K
80
69

Mochyn Du/Black Pig Press
Pant Mawr, Llansawel, Llandeilo, Carms.

First Published 1978

This Collection © Satish Kumar 1977
ISBN 0 906180 02 3

All rights reserved

Cancelled from
Gladstone's Library
2 4 JUL 2024
GLADSTONE'S
LIBRARY

Made and printed in Great Britain

137660

To Kishore

Illustrated by Amy Tiffany

Photographs: Cover and Page 154 by Hilary Evans
Page 136 by The Observer

Contents

Photographs

Introduction

One night near midnight a journalist was watching television, sitting in a modern living room in a flat on the thirteenth floor. He was living there not because he planned or wished to do so, but still he was living there. What I was saying on the television offered him an escape route from his seemingly comfortable but suffocating life.

Next morning he phoned me. "I am Tim Wilson. I saw you on television last night and I want to meet you." He came to see me the same afternoon. "I think there is a book in your thought and life." Tim said. "I can't write English" was my reply. Tim was persistent, so we agreed that every day for a few hours I would tell my story to him. He taped it and transcribed the story each day, but before it was completed I left for India by car. Tim's persistence brought him up to Belgrade for about four weeks to get the whole story out, and he did manage to complete it up to that point in my life.

When he heard that I was back in Europe he contacted me again and came to stay with me for another few weeks in a small village in West Germany where I was then living. What follows is not written word but spoken word, and therefore if the reader finds it lacking in style or jumping in places I hope he or she will understand. This book lay for many years in the drawer of my desk and would not have seen the light of day but for June, who went over the whole manuscript with me and filled some of the gaps and holes.

Satish Kumar

Pentre Ifan Farm
Felindre Farchog
Crymmych
Dyfed, Wales

Mother

Before I was born, while mother was still pregnant with me, she often had a dream — always the same dream. An old wise man with a long beard was riding with her on the back of an elephant into a forest. He promised to take her to a land of gold and jewels.

"Why are we on the back of an elephant?" mother asked. "Let's go on horseback so we can arrive more quickly."

The wise man said, "I don't know the way. Only the elephant knows the way."

Mother argued, "This is stupid. A horse is much more intelligent than an elephant."

The wise man replied, "It's not a question of intelligence but a question of going the right way."

Mother's dream always ended with her and the wise man riding on the elephant, never reaching their destination.

On the ninth of August 1936 I was born at four in the morning: the time of Brahma, the god of creation, a time of complete stillness, calm and peace. As the rays of the sun touch the earth, so the rays of knowledge come to the soul.

When mother consulted the brahmin, the village astrologer, about her dream, he said that I was the child of her unfulfilled wishes and that I would never have gold or jewels and that I would never reach my destination. Then, offering *ghee* (melted butter) to the fire, the brahmin named me Bhairav Dan, which means 'gift of Shiva'.

I was four years old when father died. My only memory of him, except for holding his finger and walking, was of his body wrapped in a white cloth, only his face showing, his eyes as if in deep sleep and surrounded with coconuts and flowers, lying on a wooden stretcher in the courtyard of our home. Relatives and friends of the family came from miles around, all the women wearing green saris as a sign of mourning. When they reached the beginning of our street they started wailing loudly.

Mother went into a room. In tears, one by one she removed all the precious jewellery which father had given her when they were married — golden chains, bracelets and rings, pearls, diamonds and silver bangles. She took off the pendant from her forehead, the diamond stud from her nose, her diamond earrings, her gold armlet, her belt of gold wire studded with pearls, her silver anklets and silver toe rings. She removed her yellow sari embroidered with gold and put on a plain green one. She sat on the floor in the corner of the room. For days she didn't move, she didn't speak to anybody, she didn't take food. She just stayed in the corner of the room weeping. I came to her asking,"Why are you here, why don't you come out, why don't you come to the kitchen, why don't you . . .?"

Four men took father's body onto their shoulders and carried him in a funeral procession. Outside the town they laid him on the funeral pyre. More wood and coconuts were heaped over his body and the fire was lit. Melted butter and sandalwood incense was poured onto the fire while the village priest chanted mantras*. We stood in a circle around the pyre until the fire died. Next day the ashes were collected and then taken by my brother to Benares to be offered to the river Ganges.

I followed my mother like her own shadow. I went wherever she went. I was part of her body. She breast-fed me until I was two years old. She massaged my body daily with sesame oil. I slept in the same bed as mother and always ate off her plate. Mother rose at four in the morning and meditated for 48 minutes, the prescribed period in the Jain religion, the religion of our family. She sat alone on the verandah with the glass sandtimer, and meditated partly in silence and partly chanting the Jain Mantra of Surrender:

> I surrender to the One who is Englightened
>   and therefore has no enemy
> I surrender to the Released Spirit
> I surrender to the Wise Guru
> I surrender to the Spiritual Teacher
> I surrender to the Seekers of Englightenment

She chanted it one hundred and eight times on a bead necklace.

During her meditation she took a daily vow of limitation, such as today I will eat rice, lentils, wheat, mango, melon, cucumber, cumin, chilli, salt, water, milk, butter and nothing else. Today I will not travel more than ten miles, and only towards the East.

At dawn she ground the flour by hand with a stone mill or churned butter from yoghurt. At sunrise mother milked our cows and the water-

---

* *mantras are verses from Hindu scriptures*

14

buffalo. Then she would turn the animals out for the cow-herd to take them to graze for the day.

We were a large family — my three brothers, my four sisters, my uncle and great uncle, their sons, wives and grandchildren all lived in the house. If we were all together, the number of us would be about forty. Breakfast was generally a glass of milk, tea and coffee were never allowed.

The family would eat the midday meal from eleven o'clock onwards. Mother would make sure that each member's taste was cared for. Eating in our family was never a social occasion, it was an act of personal satisfaction. No conversation was allowed while eating. Though she limited her own appetite, mother would prepare for each of us our favourite foods — but food was also her weapon to punish us for disobedience. For all of us mother was the only mother, the head of the household, my cousins would call their own mother 'sister'.

The family was strictly vegetarian — no meat, no fish, no eggs. About fifteen hundred years ago some wandering monks of the Jain religion came to my ancestral village of Os. They preached complete adherence to the principle of *ahimsa* (not harming any living creature). My ancestors were Rajputs, they belonged to the caste of Kshatriya (the warriors). They ate meat, they collected the taxes and they were soldiers of the King. The monks awakened them to renounce all killing. The monks converted the whole village into pacifists and vegetarians. The King granted the Oswals (the people of Os) leave from the army on the ground of conscience, but they had to step down from the warrior caste to the traders caste. He appointed my ancestor as Treasurer to the King and since then we have born the name Sethia (the treasurer).

Just before sunset, in common with Jain practice, we would eat the evening meal. As we ate I would hear cowbells ringing as our cows found their way home at 'cow-dust time.' Our two cows, a brown and a white one, would come into the courtyard and I would run to prevent the cow going to her calf while mother prepared the milk bucket. Mother would allow the calves to suckle a little before she milked the cow and she would leave milk in the udder for the calves to finish. Then she would milk the waterbuffalo which was harder to milk but mother always kept at least one because buffalo milk is rich in butter. While she was milking she would let me feed the camel. The milk was always boiled, she never allowed us to drink unboiled milk. After boiling,

15

mother would give me some cow's milk to drink and also to anyone else who wanted to drink. The boiled buffalo milk would be set for yoghurt.

After father's death, mother spent more and more time with the wandering Jain monks. She would leave the animals with a neighbour and she and I would go off in our camel cart with pots, pans, food and bedding. For several weeks we would accompany the monks and hear their story-telling and reading from the scriptures, following them from one village to another. The monk's life is a life of continuous movement, a flow like a river. These monks have no permanent place. They walk from village to village, starting after sunrise and walking a few miles. They can spend only a few days in a village — begging their food, and sleeping in houses which disciples vacate for them. It is only during the monsoon months that they can stay long in one place.

When I was seven a group of monks came to spend the *chaturmas* (the four monsoon months) in our town. The news of the monks' arrival travelled by word of mouth and a group of people, including mother and myself, went along the desert path to greet them, singing songs of welcome — "Today the sun is golden because our gurus are coming with a message of peace . . ."

Suddenly out of the sand and bushes, I saw three monks in their white robes walking barefoot and carrying a few belongings on their backs. They were walking fast, their faces impassive to the crowds around them. I had to run to keep up. People had gathered in the courtyard of the house where the monks were staying to hear their first sermon. One of the monks, monk Kundan, who was sitting on a table, started speaking.

"Seekers, we have come to show you the path to liberate your soul. The soul is wrapped up in good and bad *karma** which imprison it. We have to break away from these illusions. Sometimes we have to leave everything we know and love, mother, father, wife, children. These relationships are the expression of possessive love that destroys, maims and kills, rather than the expression of divine love that sustains the universe and has life in all of us . . ."

At the end, men of the town went up to the monks, put their heads on their feet and asked for blessings. I went up to monk Kundan.

* *Karma — The inexorable law of retribution for evil deeds and reward for un-selfish behaviour*

16

He looked deep into my eyes and talked with me. I asked him if he would come to my home to receive food. He enquired the way. When I got home Mother said he wouldn't come because it was the first day and he would have been invited to many homes. I insisted we wait to eat and keep the doors open, since monks can only come into a house with an open door. I kept running out into the street to look for him. Nobody else thought he would come. After some time I saw him coming.

He said to me, 'We're going to spend four months here, will you come every day to receive knowledge from us?'

At that time I was learning to read and write from our brahmin, astrologer and teacher, so I went to the monks in the morning, and in the evening. The early morning encounter with the monks is called *darshan* — a glimpse of a holy face which is to purify and inspire. The monks would be in meditation, sitting on the verandah wrapped in their cotton shawls. In the evenings I went to hear monks telling the story of Rama, which was told little by little over a period of about ten weeks. Fifty or sixty people from our town gathered to hear it every night. The narration of Rama's story was a combination of entertainment and religion. We sat listening in darkness — the monks do not use any kind of light. 'Dark is beautiful, not to be burnt,' they said.

One evening, cool after the monsoon rain, before the story-telling began, the senior monk, Kundan, talked to mother and me. He said that there was a line on my foot, the lotus line, "we think he is the reincarnation of a spiritual soul. He looks and behaves like a spiritual person. For many generations no-one from your family has offered themselves as a monk. Out of eight children, surely you could contribute one?"

It was dark. I couldn't see mother's face.

Next day monk Kundan said to me, "If you become a monk, the people will come to listen to your preaching, they will bow their heads at your feet. You will go to heaven and after heaven to nirvana."

"What is nirvana?" I asked.

He said, "No death."

That impressed me — no death. Father's death had created a deep question in my mind. I couldn't understand where he had gone. Whenever I asked mother about him, she said I asked too many questions and didn't answer, so I used to ask the monks about what happened after death. Monk Kundan described human life in *samsara*, (the everlasting round of birth and death) and the role of the monks who alone can free the individual from it. He showed me a picture.

A man lost in the forest was being chased by a wild elephant. The man climbed a tree and grabbed hold of a branch, but the elephant started to shake the tree with his trunk, trying to pull it out of the ground. Under the tree was a water hole in which there were poisonous snakes with their heads in the air, hissing. Sitting on the branch to which the man was clinging were two rats, a white and a black rat, symbolising day and night. Just above the man was a wild bees' nest. When the elephant shook the tree, the bees flew out and started stinging the man all over, but from the bee hive drops of honey trickled down into the man's mouth, and the honey was deliciously sweet. Flying angels asked the man if he wanted to be rescued. He said, "Yes, yes, but could you wait for this drop of honey which is just coming, see it's coming, just wait . . ." The angels flew away. The man shouted after them, "It's coming, wait . . ."

He also showed me pictures of heaven and hell. Heaven was full of exotic flowers, beautiful men and women wearing rich clothes and fabulous jewellery, palaces, thrones, aeroplanes in which angels flew. He told me that those who didn't become monks went to hell for thousands and thousands of years. The pictures of hell terrified me — tortures, bodies being cut up and boiled in cauldrons of hot oil . . . Because he had been a business man, I could see my father in hell being tortured, cut up and fried. I could not eat or play the pictures of hell made me shiver. If I went into business I would go to hell to, I thought.

It was October, cool and dry, and the monsoon was over. The night before the monks left I couldn't sleep. After sunrise mother was busy looking after the animals, but I went to see the monks. A crowd had gathered to see them off. Some people walked with them and I also followed. At the next village they stopped. Monks went to beg food for themselves — it was considered wrong to give it to a non-monk and the other followers didn't know I had come alone, so nobody worried about me. I was very hungry. It was the first time I had been out of the town without mother. At home mother was worried. She searched everywhere. Eventually someone told her that they had seen me following the monks. She walked the ten miles to the village in the evening and found me.

"Did you eat?" she asked.

I said, "I haven't eaten, I'm hungry, give me some food."

She said, "You're stupid. Why didn't you ask someone to give you some food?" I didn't tell mother that I wanted to be like the monks.

Mother came from a peasant family and wasn't happy unless she did some farming. Every year when the monsoon came, she would hire about four acres of land — always on the west side of town so that when we went to it in the morning the hot sun would be on our backs, and in the evening when we returned, the sun would again be on our backs. Just after the first rain of the monsoon mother employed a neighbour to plough with our camel but all the other work she did herself. We planted maize, mung (green beans), sesame, water melons, sugar melons, marrows, horseradish, carrots and gram peas. Mother prepared almond sweet for me and took it with us for our lunch. When the water melons started to ripen, mother and I would dig holes in the sand for the melons and cover them with sand so that birds and animals didn't eat them and they could ripen on the plant. They would grow big and sweet and red inside, weighing up to 30 pounds. We would take them home on the camel cart and store them for the winter. Mother would dry most of the vegetables so that we had vegetables all the year round.

One morning mother and I rode out on our camel to the land. The maize crop was ripe. We built a small hut with wood and rushes. There we could sleep and protect the crop while we were harvesting.

Mother asked me why I looked so sad? I couldn't answer. She said: "You don't listen properly, you're not interested in playing any more. Look at the other children, see how gay and cheerful they are while you mope around, you miserable little soul."

When I was eight, the head of our sect of the Jain order, the 'guru', Acharya Tulsi, spent the monsoon months in our town. Two rich families gave their homes to the guru for this period. Canvas tents were put up in the courtyards where the people could go to hear the guru and receive his blessings. Mother took me to welcome the guru. I saw Tulsi walking towards us across the desert. He was plump and

19

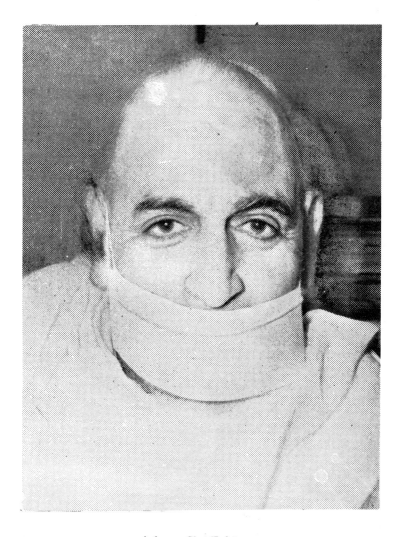

Acharya Shri Tulsi

short but his eyes were shining like big lights. His face was fair, calm and peaceful. Three deep lines cut across his forehead. His brows were bushy and black. His ears were long as I had seen on the statues of gods and hair grew on the outer edge denoting wisdom. His arms were long too, which meant a man of many resources. His step was firm. He alone among the monks wore snow white clothes. All other monks carried bags on their backs, he alone was burden free. He walked like a lion. He raised his hands to bless us.

After the guru walked forty monks, then sixty nuns, then the male disciples, then the women. Men and women sang welcoming songs

The sun is golden today
The guru comes to our town
O men and women gather together
And sing the songs of happiness
Now we can swim the ocean of *samsara*

The monks and nuns walked with their eyes on the ground and remained silent. They looked like glorious angels in their robes. Through the clouds of dust I looked for any monk I might know. I saw monk Kundan. He smiled and raised his hand. I felt as if the guru had come to rescue me from death.

A few weeks later monk Kundan took me to the guru. Normally the guru remained aloof, beyond reach, and talked only at sermon times but this day he looked at me with his kind and gentle eyes.

I said, "The monks have told me that they feel something spiritual in me, a link with my previous life, and that I should become a monk."

The guru replied, "A monk's life is very hard. You may have spiritual links from a previous life, but in order to continue these links in this life you have to gather strength and dedication."

His words reverberated in my mind. I felt I belonged to the guru. He would take me to *nirvana*, (enlightenment) he would give me light. I longed to put myself in his hands.

I stopped going to school and sometimes didn't even go home to eat. I no longer saw my friends and playmates. At night I walked in the desert thinking of Tulsi. In moonlight the sand shone like silver and sometimes I slept on the sand. During the day I wandered around. The town was quiet. Near the well under a pipal tree sat a rich fat man smoking his hookah. Shepherd children rested under the trees with their goats and sheep. In the market place the women were buying monsoon fruits and vegetables and chatting. But all this did not attract me.

As every morning, mother was making butter. She sat on the verandah by a pillar with the yoghurt in a large clay pot in front of her. She pulled a wooden pestle backwards and forwards with a rope, gradually churning the yoghurt, dividing it into butter and buttermilk. The beautiful sound of butter churning woke me up. I went to mother and sat by her. I wanted to tell her of my meeting with the guru, but I just sat looking at the butter-making, waiting for the butter to come, with a *chappati* (a flat bread) in my hand.

Impatient I interrupted mother, "The butter is ready, it's coming, give it to me."

She said, "It isn't ready − wait."

I looked into the pot and pointed to some bubbles, "See, it has come."

Feeling my anxiety, she gave me some butter which was still not quite ready. After a while she said, "What's the matter with you, little one?"

I said, "I want to become a monk."

Mother was shocked. There was silence. Then she said, "I was dreading the day you would say this. But my son you're too young. You can become a monk later on."

She burst into tears. We didn't speak any more about it.

The brahmin came to our house to ask why I wasn't going to school. Mother told him that I wanted to become a monk and she could not prevent it. She told him of a vow she had made when I had small-pox at the age of five. (Smallpox is a deity called *'mata'* (mother) so as not to offend her, and if someone has smallpox we say, "Mother has come into the body". Every year a special day is dedicated to her when the family doesn't cook but eats the previous day's food. If *mata* is offended, she is supposed to come into the body in the form of small-pox). When I had smallpox mother said, she thought she had done something wrong and every day she prayed to *mata*, "Please leave my beloved son." In spite of herbal medicines, I became so ill that mother feared I would die. She promised *mata*, "If you leave my son, I will never stand in the way of him leading a religious life." From the day she made this vow, I started getting better.

The brahmin was angry with mother saying, "Your son is not an animal to be sacrificed. You'll regret it later on."

Although the brahmin was very close to our family, he was a Hindu not a Jain, and therefore mother couldn't trust him on religious matters.

I listened to mother and the brahmin arguing. She said that if she broke her vow, *mata* might come again and this time kill me. One day she said to me, "Bhairun, the thought of your becoming a monk grieves me but I have given my word to Mata. I will not interfere. You must decide for yourself." And then she burst into tears again. My decision was already made.

Together with mother and some prominent people of the town, I went to the guru to make a formal request to become a monk.

The guru said, "You should wait. Think more. You're going to become a monk for your whole life and there will be no turning back."

After a week I went to ask him again. Again he said, "Wait more."

After many pleas he said, "I accept to consider your request and I will ask monk Kundan to teach you and examine your intention properly."

A month later Kundan reported to the guru that I would make a good monk. I went to the guru with my final request.

He pronounced, "On the last day of the monsoon I will make you a monk."

I was happy but my family was in tears. The leading members of the Jain community made elaborate arrangements to celebrate my initiation into monkhood. There were dinner parties – at least one every day for the six weeks that were left till the end of the monsoon. Sometimes a hundred people would gather to eat with me. People gave me whatever I wanted to eat, to drink, to wear, to see. A white horse and horseman took me wherever I wanted to go. This horseman was famous in the community for his skill, and when he led the horse it would dance. We went to the main squares in the surrounding villages and he would announce that I was the boy who was to become a monk and that everyone was invited to the ceremony, and the horse would dance for the people with me on its back. I wore pearl necklaces, diamond earrings, golden chains and rings. I was dressed in silk and satin. On my head was a silk turban and round it a jewelled band and pendant. One quarter of mother's jewellery was made up into five hundred silver rings and a hundred golden rings, and on every ring my name was inscribed. I gave them away to people I met — friends, neighbours, and relatives — as a remembrance of my becoming a monk.

The family were required to give their written consent and also to be present at the ceremony. My brothers and brothers-in-law were not convinced that a boy of nine should become a monk. My eldest brother said "O mother, have your wits left you? In your unstable emotional state you made a promise to mata but you did not say that he would become a monk at such a tender age. It's not too late even now, we can at least postpone this event for a few years." Mother was upset and confused but still sure that she should not stand in my way. She put her trust in the guru. The Brahmin came again full of anger, his eyes were red and he was biting his lips. I was frightened that he might make her change her mind. I sat outside the room praying, "O Lord Mahavir, give strength to my mother to stand up to him and don't let this pagan brahmin make trouble." I heard him shouting, "In your old age you have lost all sense. I have never seen you do anything which is not right, but now some demon possesses you and you are letting this foolish child take this difficult decision alone. He is not destined to be a monk. I know his horoscope and I know his stars. I tell you that he cannot stay a monk, so stop him now." Hearing his words my heart beat fast. I put my ear to the door to hear mother's reply. "I have never gone against your advice. I have never said no to you but in this matter I must follow my guru and if he agrees to Bhairan's wish then I dare not say no". The Brahmin stamped his foot. "Your Guru is a fanatic to make children monks at the innocent age of nine. Go to Hell if you wish to, but don't blame me that you were not warned." He walked out in fury and I heard my mother sobbing. I went in to mother to reassure her, "Mother, don't cry. Our guru is kind and will look after me well. Monk Kundan said that I will have no difficulties and you can come to have my *darshan* (glimpse of a holy face) and hear my sermons and I will bless you and the whole family will be blessed." Mother hugged me tight and said "my son I will not pull you back into the darkness of Samsara. You have my consent."

On the day of my initiation a message arrived to say that one of my brothers couldn't leave Bihar.

The guru said, "All members of the family must be here to give their consent. If your brother cannot come, I cannot make you a monk."

It was a disaster. I suspected that this was a trick on the part of my brothers to prevent me from following my true path. Openly they did not dare to oppose my mother, but maybe this way they could stop me.

Mother sent a telegram asking my brother when he could be present. He telegraphed back, "In two weeks."

I went with a special request to the guru that all my family could be present in two weeks and could he wait till then to make me a monk. The monks ought to have left immediately after the end of the monsoon, but the guru agreed to extend his stay.

On the day of the ceremony I got up just before dawn. My sisters and mother rubbed my body with a paste of turmeric powder, sesame oil and lentil flour, then they washed me with flower-scented water. My head was shaved except for a tuft of hair in the middle. Mother and my sisters dressed me in ceremonial dress.

An hour after sunrise the procession arrived at our house – fifteen horses, twenty camels, a band, singers and more than a thousand people. The time had come to depart.

Mother put her arms round me then burst into tears, "I'll be alone, who will be with me . . .?"

I climbed on the horse. Mother walked in the procession behind me and we went round the town making it known that I was going to be made a monk that day and asking all people to come and be witness to it. Three hours after sunrise we reached an open place in the centre of the town. There on a high dais was the guru surrounded by all his monks and nuns. They were wearing simple white seamless robes. Sitting in the open space was an assembly of thousands of towns' people – women to one side and men to the other. In between the men and the women was a long pathway with a carpet over it. I stepped down from the horse and walked to the dais.

I bowed my head on the guru's feet and said, "I have come to you to receive knowledge, I have come to search for a new life, I have come to seek *nirvana*. I am ready and I beg you to accept me. O my guru, will you lighten the darkness, will you purify my sinful soul?"

The guru answered, "I am here in this world to give knowledge of *nirvana*, I am here on this earth to help people find light, I am here to help people search for their soul and find liberation. If you want to do this, I am ready to help you."

I went behind a curtain to change my clothes. One by one, I

handed over the jewellery, money and clothes to my family, and they gave me three wooden bowls for begging food and water. My brother came forward with a white silk robe which I put on.

I went back to the guru and said, "Nothing belongs to me. I renounce everything, I am ready to leave this world, I am ready to follow your path."

The guru declared in a loud voice, "My disciple, I accept you. The first thing you have to practise is *ahimsa* (total non-violence). Respect all that is living and all creation. Do not hurt any person — neither plants, nor water, nor fire, nor air. Practise truth. Do not steal. Practise celibacy. Do not touch money nor think of it, have no possessions and live in poverty. Lastly, surrender your mind, your heart, your soul, your will to the guru. Live in obedience."

"I accept."

The guru called to my relatives "This member of your family has come to me to find light, to find truth and *nirvana*. (freedom from the cycle of death and birth). I have accepted him to be my disciple and to live with me. Do you agree?"

Mother and my family said, "We have no more claim on him."

The guru went on, "He is no more your son, your brother, your relative. He is no longer part of your society."

My brother read out the written statement signed by all the family which ended by saying, "We are fortunate that a member of our family has the wisdom and the understanding to accept this challenge and to search for a new life."

The guru turned to my family and took the document. I climbed the steps and put my head on the guru's feet. He held my head in one hand and with the other plucked the remaining hair from my scalp. A blaze of fire shot through my whole body.

The guru said, "You have no past, you no longer belong to this world."

Guru

In the morning the *Guru* said to me, "O beloved of the gods now you have become a monk and therefore when you walk keep your eyes on the ground before you. Stand relaxed only on that ground which is devoid of living beings. Clean it before you sit or sleep on it. Speak in a language which is good, short and restrained. You will have no fixed abode. You will not possess more than thirty yards of cloth at a time. You will not use cushions or quilts. You will not drink water, eat or take medicine at night. You will not sleep in the day. You will not travel by train or automobile or any other means of transport but your feet. You will not wear shoes or slippers. You will carry all your belongings yourself. You will not shave your head or chin with a razor but pluck out your hair and beard."

Then the guru called Monk Kundan and said to him "You sowed the seeds of renunciation of the world in Bhairav. Now I put him in your care to train him in the rituals so that he can follow the path of Mahavir, our Lord. Teach him the true knowledge, true vision and right action." The guru turned to me and said, "Follow the instructions and commands of Monk Kundan. He is the wisest among our wise monks. His soul is pure and his life is humble." I placed my head on Kundan's feet and from that moment I followed him. My day began about two hours before sunrise with learning how to meditate. For one hour I remained sitting in the lotus positon, silent and still. I wore a cloth folded eight times across my mouth to prevent any violent exhalation of breath which might hurt the air or any organisms in it. This cloth could only be removed to enable me to eat, and while eating I could not speak. In the morning and evening I learned to inspect my clothes and belongings (Blanket, begging bowls and manuscripts) to see that no ants or insects had got into them. I was instructed to walk slowly and gently, always being careful not to tread on any insects or plants. At night when I could not see clearly, I did not go outside; and if I walked within the house, I swept the floor in front of me with a broom of soft wool. The doors were always left open so that no creature could be trapped as they closed, and I slept on the floor wrapped in a blanket.

As a new monk I was favoured and did not beg for food. When the other monks brought food, the guru was the first to receive it, then myself and the other young monks. Every scrap of food had to be eaten. I would clean my bowl with a small piece of unleavened bread, wash it with some water and then drink the water. In the evening the other monks ate the remainder of the morning meal, but someone would go out specially to beg a hot meal for the guru, and I was also allowed to take hot food with him. If the guru offered us some of his food we all wanted it because he had touched it. If after drinking from a cup of milk the guru passed it to me, I would feel that I was blessed. We all would wait for a kind look from the guru. After a meal a rug was put down on the floor on which the guru would walk. Sometimes he would rest his hand on my shoulder, but I had to be careful not to tread on the rug as I went along with him.

According to the rule of the monks, I didn't wash my clothes. I wore the same clothes until they wore out. I never took a bath nor cleaned my teeth. One day sitting by the guru I scratched my hair and fleas fell out. The guru looked at me and said, "You have fleas, it doesn't matter. You must remember that you have taken a vow that you will not hurt any creature, even a flea. Take the fallen fleas back and put them in your hair so that they will not die."

"But they irritate me — I cannot bear them."

"It's a test of your endurance," he said. "Don't think of the body at all."

I accepted his command.

And so we lived, walking from village to village, sometimes staying one night, sometimes two or three. My feet were sore and blistered and full of thorns. The desert produces a thorn sharp and strong as a needle which I could carry to take out these splinters. It is said: 'The thorn can be removed only by a thorn.'

The guru gave me daily teachings in the Jain scriptures. I was being trained to answer questions. People would come to discuss and debate with the guru, and I would listen. There was criticism of the practice of making young boys and girls into monks and nuns. The guru would present me as an example of a young monk who was totally committed to the spiritual life. When we went for morning walks he would sit with me near a tree and say, "Start speaking now. Imagine you have two thousand people in front of you, and you have to convince them of your belief."

A few months after I entered the monkhood, monk Kundan came to the guru. He was in his mid-seventies, toothless with a pale and wrinkled face. After a few minutes' silence he said, "I'm growing old. My body doesn't work any more. I'm unable to practise all the obligations and duties of a monk's life. I beg you to allow me to die."

"I understand your great desire," the guru said. "If a monk lives, he leads a good life; if he dies, he embraces a better life."

"I wish to undertake the practise of *Santhara*" (a fast unto death) Kundan said.

"The fast unto death, is a path of pain and suffering."

"I am ready for pain and suffering."

"If that is your wish," said the guru, "This evening I will announce your decision."

At sunset all the monks and lay disciples gathered to receive the guru's blessing. The guru asked Kundan to stand. There was a smile of happiness and the courage of faith on Kundan's face.

The guru spoke loudly, "Death is not something to be afraid of. It is the soul changing its garments. The soul leaves this body and takes a new one. But through *Santhara* the monk prepares himself for *moksha* (ultimate salvation). I am very glad to see monk Kundan embracing death. I bless him."

During his fast I went to Kundan and sat beside him.

"The guru said that you will go to the land of angels."

"It's true," Kundan said calmly.

"No one has returned from there to tell us whether it exists or not."

"Why do you have doubts, my young monk?"

"Hundreds of monks have died and gone to heaven, but not one of them has returned. I want you to come and tell me whether heaven exists."

"The angels of heaven live a very superior life. Heaven is very far from here, and this world is full of dirt, smells and ugliness. Angels cannot bear the atmosphere of this planet, they cannot stand the filthy air of this earth."

"Aren't angels powerful enough to break through the barriers and come for a few moments to tell us or even send us a message from heaven?"

Kundan said, "I understand your desire and I promise you that if

I can I'll come to you."

Kundan asked me to sing a song which he had taught me:

"O Lord Mahavir bless me with death at the moment when I am filled with the thought of you and when I have no worldly desires, no attachment with my body and no fear of death."

He wanted me to sing this song again and again which I did. He said "Our guru is very kind. He kept me always with him. Only once did he send me away and that was last year when I came to spend the monsoon months in the town of your birth. There I found you, a diamond in the sand. So I told our guru and when you became a monk I felt my last mission had been accomplished."

After twenty-three days of complete fast Kundan died. The Jain community was happy to hear this news. I was sad. The monks said he had conquered the fear of death. I went to the room where his body had been placed. I looked at his face. I felt he had gone somewhere and might come back — in the night, in a dream, or could there be some signal that I might not recognise?

Dressed in yellow silk robes, Kundan was sat on a throne decorated with gold and red. He was carried on the shoulders of the lay disciples to the cremation ground, and on the way followers threw money for the poor. Then his body was burnt with dried coconuts, sandalwood and butter.

My hair was growing. Unwashed and uncombed, it stood on my head like a bush. Soon after sunrise on the appointed day, I prepared myself for the celebration of suffering. I went to the guru and he told me that his own brother, who was very gentle, would pluck my hair. He told me a story.

"Long ago a young monk like you stood still in meditation in a cremation ground in the wilderness. While he was there, his worldly father-in-law saw him and in anger wished to take revenge for the desertion of his daughter. So he took wet earth and made a crown on the monk's head and within it he placed the burning embers from a fire. But the young monk didn't move. He died standing and achieved *moksha* (ultimate salvation).

"In comparison to this," the guru said, "What you will suffer when your hair is removed is little and I'm confident that you will endure it bravely."

I bowed my head on the guru's feet and he laid his hand on me. I went to his brother who was waiting with a drink of almond paste mixed with honey and milk. I drank it, then sat on the floor with my head between his knees. He gripped my head tightly and held my neck with his left hand, then with his right hand he took hold of some hair and tugged it out with a quick sweeping movement until every hair was removed from my head. Fellow monks stood near me and sang inspirational songs. My head was scarred and bleeding. My hair and its fleas were wrapped around my leg and tied and knotted tight so that the fleas could have their food from my body. They remained there until the fleas were dead.

One evening after the burning heat, a few drops of rain had fallen and people gathered in the village square to welcome the monsoon. We were on the verandah of a mud hut in meditation. I heard the sounds of drums and songs and, still sitting in my lotus position, I could see dancers passing in the distance. I tried to return to meditation but without success. Later a monk spoke of the dancers. The guru looked up with a blank face and I realised that he had heard and seen nothing. His meditation had not been broken. I went to the guru as he was preparing to go to sleep and asked him what I should do to experience true meditation.

He put his hand on my head. I felt a sense of relief in his touch.

"Do you know why you are a monk?" the guru asked me.

"Not clearly," I replied.

"The monk's life is a way to achieve *moksha* — total liberation." he said.

"My desire to achieve *moksha* is growing, but I am not sure of the path."

The guru replied, "Do not doubt. As long as you are caught up in doubting, thinking and questioning, you will not be able to experience the spiritual life. Submit your thoughts, your sorrows, your unhappiness to me. I am the ship to cross this wild sea of *samsara* (cycle of birth and death). Pronounce the mantra of surrender a thousand times a day, lose yourself in the deep sound of it. Fast on alternate days. This will give you better concentration. Only renouncing house, property, parents and possessions is not enough. You must also renounce your own will."

One day after the guru had given his morning sermon, he called me and said, "It is the holy duty of a monk to go and beg for food. We eat food not to build the body nor to satisfy the palate, but to enable the body to practise *dharma* (the fulfillment of right action). Today I send you to beg. Do not knock at the door of a house when the door is closed. Go to a house where the doors are open. Take only from people who are giving happily. The food should not be specially prepared for you and you should not announce your going beforehand. You will meet many people who will refuse to give food, but do not take offence. Bless those who give and those who do not give alike. By begging you will learn humility. If a person offers you three chappatis (flat bread), take one; if you are offered one, take a quarter. No one should be able to say that they have gone without because you have taken. Ask people to share their food with you and only to give what they are able to be without and not to cook more after you have gone. Fill your bowl from many places, but beg only once a day."

After a silence the guru went on, "Begging should not be easy. Often it may be necessary to make conditions which unless fulfilled prevent us from accepting food. This enables us to practice endurance. Our Lord Mahavir, the founder of our religion two thousand five hundred years ago, made a vow that he would only accept food from a princess. This princess should have been sold and be chained by the foot so that one foot was outside the house and one foot inside. There should be tears in her eyes and she should offer soaked beans in a bamboo plate. For many days Mahavir fasted, but at last he came to a rich man's house and sitting in the doorway he saw a woman whom he recognised as the daughter of a defeated king. She had been bought by a rich man who had been called away on business and left her chained. When she saw Mahavir coming, she forgot her sorrows and smilingly said, "O Lord Mahavir, in my pain and misfortune you have found me. Teach me the way to liberation. I have nothing but soaked beans to offer you. Accept them and give me your blessing." All the conditions of his vow were fulfilled except that the princess was smiling so Lord Mahavir turned away. Then the princess wept — "Everyone has deserted me and even you refuse my offering. To whom can I look in this world?" Mahavir turned his head and seeing tears in her eyes, he put both hands together and received the food.

Now you must go and fulfil your *dharma*. Just as the honey bee goes from flower to flower and harms none, so you should go from house to house taking little."

The guru gave me a square of cloth with the four corners tied together. In it there were three bowls — one for liquids such as milk, one for vegetables, one for dry foods like nuts, rice, chappatis or sweets. Then he told me and the other monks to which area we should go so that not more than one monk went to any house.

I went to a house. There was a large family and on my arrival all the members of the family gathered together. I checked that the food was not touching fire, that there was no unboiled water or raw vegetables and that the people giving me the food were not wearing flowers nor standing on grass or other plants. I made sure that the food had not been prepared for me.

One young man said, "You are strong and healthy. Why don't you monks work and produce food?"

I didn't answer. The women told me not to listen. They were happy to share their food with me. They offered me cream, almonds and milk-sweets, and I took a little. I went to ten houses and I brought sufficient food for several monks. First I offered to the guru and he took some and made me happy, and the rest I shared with other monks and the other monks shared with me.

One cold morning a monk complained to the guru that he had gone to bring water from a house: "I saw a begging bowl in front of a room. I couldn't understand how a begging bowl could be there, so I waited outside. After a few minutes this monk appeared and a woman followed him. Therefore I believe that he has broken his vow of chastity."

The accused monk confessed, "I went for food to the home of a disciple. The husband of the woman was not there. She was beautiful. When I saw her smiling face I forgot myself and I forgot that I should leave her immediately after receiving food. I started talking and during the talk I kissed her and asked her whether she would make love with me. She said, "How can I say no to a monk?" We started to have intercourse, but I remembered my vow and stopped before I discharged myself."

The guru declared, "If you had discharged yourself, you would have destroyed your whole monkhood and you would have had to become a monk again. But I believe you, and therefore, only six months of your monkhood are destroyed and all those who became a monk during that period will take precedence before you."

The guru asked us not to speak of this to anyone and said "Bhartrihari realised long ago that the love of woman is part of the world of illusion."

"Please guru tell us how he came to this realisation."

"Listen my monks. In the kingdom of King Bhartrihari was a great yogi who practised self-mortification and meditation for many years. God Vishnu, being happy to observe such a great act of purification, came and said, "You have purified your soul and as a reward, take this fruit of immortality." For many days the yogi kept the fruit, not knowing how he could best use it. Then he thought, "What is the good of my body becoming immortal? I can do no good to anyone. But we have a King who is just and kind, who follows *dharma* and serves his people, if he lives forever all the people will live in peace and harmony. Who knows who will be king after Bhartrihari? And whether he will be as just and good?" So the yogi came to the king and said "O King, I give you this fruit of immortality. By Vishnu's grace, death will not touch you ever. Take it and eat it so that all living creatures may prosper under your eternal rule." The King kept the fruit. He said to himself, "How could I bear to live forever without my beloved Queen? She is beautiful and devoted. She is mother to all. She has no enemies. Let my love, Queen Pingla, be immortal." The Queen received the fruit and thanked the King but did not eat at once. She had no desire to be immortal. She longed for the love of the charioteer, who was strong and fresh. The Queen spoke to the charioteer in a soft voice. "You are young and there is no match for your body. Eat this fruit and let your youth and beauty last forever." The charioteer smiled and accepted the gift. He gave the fruit to a beautiful courtesan with whom he was in love, thinking, "If such a beautiful woman lives, that will be the greatest treasure for this kingdom — beauty should never die." The courtesan came to the king and said, "I have got possession of this fruit of immortality but I am a woman who lives by selling my body. What is the good of my living forever? But you, O King, are the greatest man on this earth and if you live you will serve people, but if I live I will corrupt them. Take it and eat it." Deeply shocked, the king took the fruit. His eyes were opened. His illusions were broken. He realised that all that which he had called 'love' was merely a mirage. He said nothing, spoke to no-one, stood up, left the throne, left the palace, renounced the Kingdom, and did not look for one moment back to his beautiful women and the world of pleasures. He went to the forest, searched for the yogi and when he found him, he surrendered himself at his feet. He became a wanderer, a *sadhu*, stopping at people's homes and begging his food. Once as he was passing his former palace he sang, 'O mother Pingla, there is a yogi standing at your door, would you give him a piece of bread?' The queen was over-joyed to hear his voice and said, 'O my king, O my husband, remove those robes of a beggar monk and come back. Once again be my king, be my husband and be my lover.' Bhartrihari replied, 'O mother Pingla, truly there is no husband, nor no life. In reality there is no mother, nor father. We were born alone and we shall die alone.'

So the guru concluded, "never forget the last words of Bhartrihari, "For whom I longed, she longed not for me, and whom she loved, he loved not her, and whom he desired, she desired someone else. Shame on me, shame on you, shame on him, shame on her. Shame on sexual desires."

One night, not long after, a monk came and sat by me. He began talking about a beautiful woman and said that he went to the guru's morning preaching just to see this woman.

"We're not supposed to look at women," I said.

"There's nothing wrong in looking at women — I am not *doing* anything." he replied.

I argued, "Our guru said that looking at women arouses passion and from passion comes desire, and desire leads to destruction of monk-hood. Therefore, it is better not to see a beautiful woman."

Then he touched my face and caressed my back and took me in his arms. He rubbed his naked body against me. He took of my clothes. I didn't resist or say a word. I had an erection but he didn't touch my penis. He just went on holding me in his arms, rubbing his body against me. There was tension. It was like playing with fire. He acted in a guilty way, afraid of breaking his purity, but unable to control himself fully. I was angry at his interference with my celibacy and ashamed that I just let him have his way without resisting.

Five years passed, learning scriptures and practising rituals. I memorised 10,000 verses in Sanskrit and Prakrit (the language of Jain scriptures). The whole Sanskrit dictionary was in my head. But was I any closer to *moksha* (salvation of soul)? The monks were busy debating whether we should continue to follow the hard ascetic path laid down by the founders of the order, or adapt to modern ways and go to the cities and meet politicians, create centres, publish books and pamphlets. The guru himself longed for modernisation. So we walked hundreds of miles to spend the monsoon months in Jaipur, the capital of Rajasthan.

When we arrived in Jaipur I fell ill. I was shivering as if I was in a sea of ice but at the same time my temperature went up to 104, my body was burning. In spite of all the monks' blankets over me I was still cold. I had malaria. The guru came to my room and pronounced long *mantras* (holy verses) for my protection. But I didn't get any better. I became weak and frightened. I was convinced that I was going to die because of bad *karma* — either sexual indulgence with the monk or some other error. I was being punished. I was not allowed to be treated by a doctor, but monks went out and begged quinine which I took with hot milk.

After I recovered I became friendly with one of our lay disciples, Keval, who was our guide and stayed with us all the time. It was the first time I had ever been to a city. Keval felt it his duty to protect us by carrying a stick which contained a sword. My guru never objected, but one day I asked him about it. The guru said, "We don't carry the sword, and Keval isn't a monk. He lives in a world of compromise." Later I asked Keval himself.

"You shouldn't concern yourself with the sword, it's my business," he answered.

"But you stay with us all the time," I said.

"This is a big city and there are all sorts of people — anything might happen. Do you think I should stand by and let something happen to you or to the guru?"

"But we believe in non-violence," I said.

"You couldn't live non-violently unless we were here to protect you."

I was confused, and asked what he meant.

"You don't produce any food because there is violence in cooking or producing food, but if we don't produce or cook, can you live in this world? If monks are to live a life without committing violence or without expecting money, there must be some people to support them."

One day Keval took us to the fountain of Galta in the mountains. I had been born and brought up in desert so when I went to Galta I sat down near the fountain and looked at it for hours. The flow of water was coming from the mouth of a stone statue of a cow. Keval had brought some cannabis leaves with him and prepared the drink *bhang* (cannabis and milk) which he then drank. The high peaks of mountains were touching the clouds and hundreds of red-faced monkeys were playing around. I had never seen so many monkeys.

"Monkeys have a special place in our life," Keval said. "They are our forefathers, and moreover the monkey-faced god, Hanuman, was the greatest devotee of Rama. Therefore, we worship monkeys."

I laughed. "You seem devoted to us monks, Keval, why do you take *bhang*?"

"It gives me an opportunity to forget about the world and be myself."

"It's forbidden by our religion," I commented.

"Yes, but from personal experience I know that when I'm high with *bhang* I'm extremely happy."

We came back quite late, and I told the guru about *bhang*, the monkeys and the abundance of beauty at Galta.

The guru said, "This is all illusion. So we monks neither admire pleasing objects nor despise the unpleasant. A monk shouldn't indulge in *maya*. We are like the lotus. Although its roots are in muddy water, the flower is always above the water. We are in the world, but we are above the world."

After Jaipur we walked to Delhi. This was the first time the guru had gone to Delhi so there were thousands of disciples from Delhi and places far from Delhi gathered there to greet us. All disciples wished to have the guru's *darshan* (a glimpse of his face) and to hear him preach.

At the same time as we were walking to Delhi from the north, Vinoba Bhave was walking from the south. Vinoba had worked closely with Gandhi in the independence movement. After Gandhi's death he had lived in an *ashram* (community) doing manual work and meditation. But after the Telangana riot of landless against landlords in which thousands of people had been killed, Vinoba had solved the immediate problem by persuading the landlords to redistribute their land to the landless. He had begun by walking from village to village, saying he would not wait for the government in Delhi to bring changes, that he would walk to every village in India to bring self-government and the abolition of private ownership of land. Within a very short time, Vinoba had collected 50,000 acres for distribution among the poor and had been joined in his campaign by hundreds of young people – doctors, lawyers, teachers and students.

Overnight Vinoba became a name on everyone's lips. Here was someone with a message of land revolution and people were voluntarily giving him their possessions and property. Nehru, then prime minister of India, invited Vinoba to Delhi, offering to fly him there in a private plane, but Vinoba replied, "I will come in my own time and as always." So he walked to Delhi, and stayed not in a hotel or official residence but in a bamboo hut near the place where Gandhi's body had been cremated, by the side of the river Jumna.

Here my guru and Vinoba met. They, the two saints, were sitting on the ground on blankets, facing each other. A hundred monks and lay disciples were gathered around them. I was sitting by my guru. I looked closely at Vinoba. He had a long white beard and no teeth, his face was scholarly and wise. His eyes half closed and peaceful. I saw this man wearing less clothes than me, but unlike me not claiming to be superior in any way – a man without a label. My guru was doing most of the talking while Vinoba listened silently. The guru asked me to stand up and briefly explain the fundamentals of the Jain religion in Sanskrit. I recited a passage from scripture then spoke in Sanskrit, glorifying the meeting of the two great souls. As I was talking Vinoba looked at me and I at him. He smiled. We talked without words.

During the eight years I had been a monk I was always with my guru. He treated me as his son and I treated him as my father. People thought I was being groomed as his successor. But I was beginning to feel overpowered by him. His answers no longer satisfied me. Ever since his decision to modernise the order, I felt he was trying to travel in two boats at the same time – denouncing the world and also seeking its recognition.

Usually monks travelled in groups of three and nuns in groups of five. I wanted to go in a small group with monk Mohan, with whom I had studied and whom I knew I could trust. Both of us went to the guru to ask his permission. "We have come to ask you to bless us and permit us to travel independently. Please assign us some place where we can spend the next monsoon months."

"My young monks. Time is not yet ripe for you to go by yourselves. You should stay with me and learn more."

I said, "I have spent many years sitting at your feet and now I want to spread the knowledge you have given me."

"I give you twenty-four hours to think. Think and re-think."

Next day we went back to the guru, saying: "We have thought a lot and still wish to go independently of you."

"You have to travel through villages where there are no disciples living, and where there'll be hostility and opposition." the guru guided us in the words of Buddha. "If people come and abuse you, think that they are only abusing you, not hitting you; if they hit you, think that they are only hitting but not wounding you; if they wound you, think that they are not killing you; and if they kill you, think that they have liberated you from this body. If you are able to follow this path, then I give you my blessing to go by yourselves and spread the religion of self-denial."

After giving his blessing, the guru asked a third monk, Chandra, to join us on our journey, and he sent us to Ratangarh. The day of leaving was full of sadness. Some monks came to the outskirts of the town to see us off, then stood and waved their hands.

We travelled in the mornings and preached in the evenings. We walked for six months through beautiful desert villages to Ratangarh. During the monsoon months I preached every morning and Mohan preached in the evenings.

The disciples, men and women, gathered together three hours after sunrise and for forty-eight minutes they would become 'time-bound monks'. They removed their stitched clothing and put on a length of cloth and covered their mouths like us. They would vow that during this period they would not think of worldly affairs nor family problems, they would commit no violence, touch no money, allow no sexual desires. It was mostly to these 'time-bound' monks and nuns that I would preach, and among them was the woman who had been my mother. She had come from Dungargarh.

I would sit on a low table, the lay disciples around me. Their

41

minds were one-pointed, concentrated and ready to receive. I would begin with the mantra of Surrender. I would read a passage from one of the thirty-two books of Jain sutras, the words of Mahavir.

All that is living wishes to live
Nothing wishes to die
Therefore killing is dreadful
And the monks free from all bonds restrain from killing

then I will elaborate it with stories, analogies and examples.

In the afternoons individual disciples would come to talk about their lives and problems or to learn scripture. In the evenings Mohan would tell Ramayana (the story of Rama) episode by episode so that it would take the whole of the monsoon months to tell.

One day a disciple offered me a book of Gandhi. I told him I wasn't allowed to read any non-religious books. Next morning as I walked through the desert to find a place for my toilet, he followed and urged me to read the book. He said that this book was religious in a deep sense and therefore there would be no wrong in reading it.

What Gandhi was saying was that religion is not religion if it does not help to solve the problems of this world, here and now. If religion takes a person away from this life and this society, then it is escapism. The search for truth is a continuous daily experience. There is no absolute or ultimate truth and the search for truth never ends. Every person's life is a kind of laboratory and every person should make experiments with truth.

Gandhi's ideas were in contradiction with my guru's teaching that as monks we should keep our backs to society and our faces towards God. According to the guru, people like Gandhi who involved themselves in the world and in politics, were 'living in darkness'. Gandhi's words increased my doubts about the monk's life. For me the rituals had become monotonous. I was thirsty for the joy of spiritual experience, but I wasn't achieving it.

When I read Gandhi it was an awakening. I talked about his ideas with Mohan. Whether it was possible for us to cut off totally from the outside world. As long as we were in the body, as long as we needed clothes, food, house, then we had to attend to these needs. It seemed that we were escaping from a reality we could not deny, shutting our eyes and pretending the rest of the world did not exist. I asked him if he was sure that we would reach heaven or *nirvana*.

I could feel Mohan also wasn't satisfied. He admitted he found the monk's life too strict and the autocracy of the guru oppressive but he said "Once you are a monk, you are a monk forever. There is no way out, we have to die as monks."

After a few days we started to open our minds to Monk Chandra. He had been a monk for a couple of years and we found him also disillusioned. We discussed the possibility of leaving the monkhood. After days of deliberation the three of us decided to leave. We knew that by leaving the monkhood we would bring sorrow and pain to the guru, but we felt we could remain monks no longer.

In the town of Ratangarh, there were two hundred families who were followers of our religion and they would make it impossible for us to break from our monkhood. So we needed a way to escape secretly and quietly. There was a woman, a poetess, who had a special relationship with the guru. In previous years she used to come and see the guru and they talked together. I used to guard the door. So there was a strange bond between us and I could trust her. I suggested to Mohan that we should see if she would help us. We were afraid to speak openly, so we sat down and wrote her a letter, asking her if she could give us some normal clothes to help us escape and enough money so that we could buy train tickets to South India, we were looking for a place without any connection with the Jain community. We gave the letter to the woman when she came to our sermon that morning.

That night I had a dream. I was standing upright in a yoga position for meditation, with one leg folded and the other on the ground. A cobra came and bound itself tightly round the leg I was standing on, from ankle to knee. Because I was standing in meditation with my eyes closed, I didn't see the snake coming, nor did I even feel it wrapping itself around my leg. Only when it started tightening its grip did I become aware of it. I opened my eyes to see the snake with its body bound round my leg, its head facing me. It opened its hood, swaying its head ready to bite. Terrified, I woke up covered in sweat.

The next afternoon the woman came. Her first reaction on reading the letter was to say, "What will the guru think?" But eventually she said, "I don't want to get involved. I don't want to encourage or discourage you. I don't want to know whether or not you are going to leave the order. However, what you have asked me to do I will do, but without being emotionally attached to my action. Come to my home to beg food."

I went to her home and she gave me a small parcel of clothes for the three of us and four hundred rupees in an envelope.

That evening we did everything as usual. At sunset we had one hour's meditation, then instead of Mohan I preached. Since this was the last day of the monsoon months, a large number of people had gathered to hear the sermon. As I sat down cross-legged I caught the eye of the woman who had given me the parcel. I thought of speaking of our dissatisfaction and the reasons for our decision to leave the monkhood. This might show my courage but I knew it would make things more complicated and delay our departure. So I began by telling a story.

A rich businessman received a call from his business a long way away and left his home and his pregnant wife, thinking he would be away for a short time. However the business was doing badly and the man was forced to stay away longer and longer. Time passed. His wife gave birth to a son who grew up without his father. The son was always asking, "Where is my father? I want to see him." When the son was nine, he insisted that he should go and see his father, so his mother arranged some bullock carts and servants to accompany him. Meanwhile the father decided that he must leave his business and travel home to see his first and only son. He also set out with a large entourage of servants and bullock carts. One night the father arrived in a certain village and moved into the top floor of a guest house. A little later the son arrived in that village and stayed in the ground floor of the same guest house. In the middle of the night the little boy had a pain in his stomach which became so bad that he couldn't sleep. He was crying. The servants of the rich businessman came down and spoke angrily with the boy's servants saying, "This crying is disturbing the sleep of our lord. Get the boy out of this place." So the boy's servants took him from the guest house and made a bed for him in a bullock cart. When the businessman got up in the morning he asked. "Who was it in the night crying? What was the matter?" He was told that it was just a little boy with a stomach pain. The businessman asked what had happened to the boy and who he was. His servants went to find out and the boy's servants told them, "It is very unfortunate that this little boy died because he was travelling to his father whom he had never seen."

O seekers, we are all on a journey. It is a hard and dangerous journey. In seeking our bodily comfort we neglect our soul. We must listen to the inner cry which is disturbing us but which we suppress. This inner cry is the source of salvation. Let me warn you, my disciples, that no outside authority can lead you to liberation. You must not be deceived by false prophets or external appearances. Even monks in their white robes can deceive themselves by blindly following the outer manifestations of the spiritual life, and by deceiving themselves they can deceive everyone . . .

When my sermon ended people came up, praised me for my words, put their heads on my feet and asked for my blessings.

By nine o'clock everyone had left except a watchman who used to sleep at the front gate of the house. I told him we would be retiring early because we weren't feeling well. We decided to make our getaway late that night when no followers were near.

Ratangarh was a small town and there was hardly any electricity or outside lights. The train to Delhi stopped there at about midnight. We chose to take that train — when the disciples came in the morning they would have no idea where we had gone.

The three of us went into the room and we put a curtain over the doorway. It was a cold night and the curtain would keep the cold out. Also the watchman would think we had gone to sleep. We put our wool brushes by the door. This was a usual indication that we didn't want any non-monks to enter our room.

It was twenty minutes' walk from the house to the station. The three of us slowly came out from the room and escaped through the back door. Everything was quiet apart from a few dogs barking and no-one could be seen in the street. We changed our clothes, and ran very fast to the station. We bought three tickets for Delhi and boarded the train.

The train slowly pulled out. Some sense of relief mingled with a fear that we might be recognised. Our heads were shaven and where we removed the strip of cloth from our mouths, there were white bands across our faces. We went to a crowded third-class compartment and slept on the luggage racks so that if there were some disciples on the train they wouldn't see us.

At Ratangarh, unknown to us, someone had got off the train in which we were now heading for Delhi. This man had come with a message from some monks in another town. After getting off the train he went straight to see us and told the watchman that he had a very urgent message which he must deliver at once. He couldn't wait until morning because he had to get back very early. He stood outside the door to our room calling out, "Are you in? Why don't you wake up? I have a special message for you. Will you get up please?" There was no answer, so eventually he poked his torch through the curtain and saw that no-one was in. He ran back to the watchman and told him. They searched the whole house frantically, every room, but they couldn't find us anywhere. Realising that perhaps the three of us had escaped, he went back to the station and asked the ticket clerk if he had seen three young people going somewhere. The clerk told him that he had sold three tickets for Delhi. Immediately the man made a telephone call to our disciples in Delhi, saying that the three of us had escaped.

As the train drew into Delhi station, we saw from the window a large number of disciples on the platform waiting for us, carefully spaced out so they wouldn't miss us. They were important people, some of the leading disciples of our order. As soon as the train stopped we jumped out of the other side and onto the railway line and ran as fast as we could away from the train. Now we thought we should have got out the stop before Delhi. Here there was no other exit except at the ticket barrier. Three disciples stood at the gate waiting. There was no way of escape. One of them was shouting, "You have committed a great sin and we cannot let you go." "We don't want to go with you," we said. "We are no longer monks, you don't have any control over us." They said on no account would they let us go and we must explain why we had tried to escape. They said, "If you won't come with us, we'll report you to the police for stealing books from the order or for running away, then you'll be in trouble. Be quiet and follow us."

We didn't know what to do and the police was a real threat to us – so we went with them. They took us to some other monks in the city who told us that the Jain community would never accept us back. Nobody would give us a job, nobody would let us marry, and if we didn't come back to the monkhood, then we would be in great trouble. Again we said that we didn't want to go back to being monks. The disciples said they would put us on a plane to the guru in Bombay. They wanted us to confess to the guru that we had committed a great sin without proper understanding and beg him to take us back. Again we were obstinate, saying that whatever happened we would not become monks again. We said to ourselves "Let's face it now," and started to gain confidence.

For a week the disciples kept us in confinement, interrogating us about why we had escaped. They wrote to our relatives asking them to come and persuade us to become monks again. Finally the monks decided to hand us over to our relatives. The person who came to see me was my brother-in-law. He said that he couldn't take me to his house and that he couldn't take any responsibility for me. He had come to advise me to become a monk again, otherwise nobody would give me anywhere to live. Eventually he decided to send me to my mother who might be able to persuade me to become a monk again.

I left Delhi feeling greatly relieved. I saw the world — the sky, the mountains, the earth, people — with new eyes and they had a new meaning for me. I felt a sense of independence. I was no longer a priest, a monk. I was just a man.

ST DEINIOL'S LIBRARY HAWARDEN

Ashram

I got off the train outside Sri Dungargarh, my birthplace, and walked three miles through the sand hills to the town. It was nine years since I had left. I passed the monsoon lake where I had played as a child, riding into the water on the backs of buffalos. I passed the sacred fig trees where I hid and threw stones which knocked off the water pots from the heads of the girls so that they got a soaking, the girls who walked to the lake in lines, dressed in their beautiful saris — red, yellow and pink.

Mother wept when she saw me. "My fortune is broken. You have committed a great sin. By coming back to this world which you renounced you are eating your own vomit."

I said, "Don't cry." My heart was wet for her.

I knew what she was thinking. If she took me back she would be breaking the law of *dharma*, if she took me back the Jain community would ostracise her, if she took me back other monks might be encouraged to leave the monkhood.

"There's no room for you here," she said. "Go back to the guru. He is the only one who can make you happy. Don't come to me. For me you are dead."

I went to my sister-in-law. She said, "Let the old lady cry." She wasn't a religious person and never went to listen to the monks. "It's not very cold," she said. "I'll give you a good blanket and you can stay outside on the verandah of the guest room in the outer courtyard."

I spent the days in darkness and indecision about what to do next. Whenever mother saw me she cried. Gone was the mother I remembered sane and strong. My leaving the monkhood made her more unhappy than even my father's death. She walked about confused and disorientated. I could hear her murmuring and in despair I sat on a bench opposite the tea shop with a sad face. A teacher from the local school came up and talked to me. He said he hadn't seen me before which seemed strange since he knew all the boys in the town. I told him I was born here and later had become a monk. He wanted to know more. He invited me to his home. He gave me some *roti* (hot bread) and vegetables to eat. In the last two weeks since leaving the monkhood, this was the first person to accept me with sympathy.

He said, "Why don't you go to Vinoba?"

"But do you think he will accept an ex-monk?"

He replied, "I don't think it matters to Vinoba. You can go to an Ashram, a community of his followers. He found me the address of an ashram in Bihar where Sadhak lived. I knew Sadhak: he had been a monk with me.

That gave me hope. At home I was depressed; mother wouldn't speak to me. I had spent all the money the woman in Ratangarh had given me. I had bought a pair of trousers and a small camera. I had also bought a sweater, and some good shoes — and I had my hair cut and oil put in it. I asked my sister, Suvati, who was living off a little money her dead husband had left, to give me enough to buy a train ticket. Although she was poor, Suvati gave me twenty-five rupees.

I left for Delhi. When I arrived I went to see Daftariji, a man who had promised to give me food and a place to stay for the night. He was a kind man. A businessman. He said "Why go so far to an ashram in Bihar, you can stay with me and I will find you a job." But after five days he found it impossible to get me a job: I had no education, no degree, no languages, no mathematics, no salesmanship, no typing nor any craft, I knew nothing. My Jain community would not give a job to an ex-monk. "You're an outsider, a misfit," he said.

By this time I had just enough to buy a ticket to Bihar. When I asked the man if he could lend me some money he said, "What guarantee do I have that you will be able to pay me back?". I discovered that giving a few days hospitality was part of his *dharma* as a businessman but giving actual cash was not.

I was to leave the following morning. All night I was worried, worried . . . I couldn't sleep. The train, the Calcutta Mail, was due to leave at eight o'clock. I had to be at the station by seven to find a place and buy a ticket. I got up at five, while the others were still sleeping. As I got up I noticed a coat. I went over and put my hand in the pocket and pulled out a hundred rupees. I thought — I don't need a hundred rupees, I need about fifty rupees to keep me going. So I took fifty.

Someone woke up.

"Are you leaving now?" he asked.

I said, "Yes, I am leaving. Thanks very much for your hospitality and all your help. Goodbye . . ."

But he decided to come with me to the station. I bought a ticket then he came to the platform and helped me find a good place. After that he went back. There was still an hour before the train left. Meanwhile the owner of the coat had got up, found the fifty rupees missing and started searching everywhere. The man who came with me to the station mentioned that I had got up very early and thought that I might have taken the money because I had spoken of having very little the day before. The man remembered that I had several notes in my purse after buying the ticket, which confirmed their suspicions, so they both came to the station, found me and threatened to call the police if I didn't return the money. I gave him his fifty rupees back, which meant that I had to travel without any money.

I arrived in Gaya early in the morning of the next day. It was too dark to go anywhere so I slept on the platform. When I began searching for the Ashram, I discovered it was about seven miles from Gaya in another small town – Bodh Gaya. I went to a rickshaw man and asked if he would drive me in exchange for my cap because I didn't have any money. He agreed.

As we were travelling the rickshaw man said, "Bodh Gaya is where Buddha received enlightenment. For fifteen years I have been taking pilgrims from all over the world to the holy temple of Buddha. My *dharma* is to bring people to Buddha." I said "I am so grateful to you for taking me without money."

He said, "Don't worry about money or even about giving your cap. Many travellers and especially pilgrims pay me very well."

When we reached Bodh Gaya we found Vinoba's Ashram. There were a few people, a few small huts, and a well for water. The man in charge was wearing white clothes and had a small beard and shaved head. I asked for Sadhak. He told me that Sadhak was working in the village of Shekhwara six miles away.

I said, "I've come from Rajasthan to see him, and also I want to work and live in the Ashram. Could you let me rest for a while, then I could walk to the village where Sadhak is."

He asked me if I had any letters or references. I said "No, but I am a friend of Sadhak."

He said, "Better you go to Sadhak straightaway."

I asked if I could leave my bag. Again he said no.

I was shy to tell him that I hadn't any money, because it might have created suspicion in his mind. I went back to the rickshaw man and told him the man I was looking for was in another village. I gave him my cap and I said "Now I will walk to that village. I cannot waste any more of your time and prevent you from earning some money."

The rickshaw driver said, "Don't worry, I will take you there without paying anything. But first get the proper name of the village so we don't get lost."

When we arrived I wanted to give him my sweater. I said, "It will make me happy – it's not for you, it's for me." He was happy. He took the sweater and left. I stood and watched him go. Yesterday in the house of a rich businessman I became a thief. But the rickshaw man who had so little cared nothing for money.

On a small couch in the sun two women were sitting and spinning cotton and there was a man with no clothes except a small linen cloth round his hips. I told them I had come to see Sadhak. The man said that Sadhak was out but would be back soon. He motioned me to sit down and we began talking. He didn't stop his spinning. The women brought some breakfast to me. I hadn't eaten anything for twenty-six hours so I was very hungry. They brought me bananas, milk and porridge. After a while Sadhak came. He had left the Jain order but hadn't changed his dress – he was still wearing a white robe but without the cloth over his mouth. I was wearing Western trousers and shirt, and the village people and children gathered to stare at me as a young modern city boy. Sadhak received me warmly and said "I heard that you had left the monks but I didn't expect to see you here. I am glad. Let's go to the village well where we can bath and talk." After nine years of not having a bath and before that living in a desert town where water was scarce, buckets and buckets of water being splashed over me was beautiful, washing away all the dirt from my body and the past. I felt like I was in a new world. We laughed and threw water over each other. We spent a long time there, with the open rice paddy fields all around.

Sadhak said, "It will be good for you to have some experience of Ashram life and the philosophy behind it. I think you should live for a while at Bodh Gaya Ashram." I said "If a few minutes encounter is anything to go by I doubt if I can be happy there. Particularly the old man . . ."

"Don't worry, he's not the only person there, and later you'll find that he is a very gentle person. Perhaps he didn't understand you."

Next evening we both walked to the Ashram. Across the fields it was only 3 miles. It was prayer time, so we joined all the members gathered together sitting on blankets on the ground. They recited a passage from the second chapter of the 'Bhagavad Gita' then they chanted the name of Rama and pronounced the eleven vows of Ashram life: Non-violence, Adherence to Truth, Non-stealing, Chastity, Poverty, Manual Labour, Right Diet, Fearlessness, Religious Tolerance, Use of locally made produce, and Rejection of Untouchability. After the prayers someone reported on the work that had been done that day. Then Sadhak introduced me, and asked me to speak. The old man was impressed with my story and told me I had come to the right place. I was accepted to stay at the Ashram for a trial period.

The Ashram is an old concept for community living and collective action. The Ashram is a place where a group of people live together in harmony. The word 'Ashram' means 'a place and people engaged in productive labour'. In an Ashram a sage, scholar or scientist, lived with his or her companions and disciples to study and experiment with the spiritual and material existence of the universe. Short- or long-term visitors and students came to learn and share the knowledge and wisdom, but everybody was required to take part in the daily activities. Whether it was gathering of wood or food, or whether it was production of shoes, clothes and books, all the activities were performed by the Ashram dwellers.

As the influence of a Hindu way of life diminished during the Muslim and British rule, the number of Ashrams diminished as well. There were a large number of strictly religious and spiritual Ashrams in the foothills of the Himalayas and along the banks of the Ganges. A few hundred of them still continue. Mahatma Gandhi revived the Ashram life in the early part of this century. He established a score of new Ashrams, where his friends and followers practised the simple way of living, combined with manual labour on the land and crafts. He reorganised educational activities by putting emphasis on learning by doing. He combined political and social work with spiritual and religious practices; self-reliance and consumption of only home-made produce became the key concept of the Ashram way of life.

Next day and every day the activity started before dawn. Brother

Dwarko beat the gong and Surendra could be heard singing Vedic mantras. We all gathered for the morning prayer: a passage from an Upanishad and a reading from some spiritual book or from Gandhi.

After the morning session, I was asked if I would prepare breakfast for the Ashram members. Although I had watched my mother cooking in my early childhood, I had never touched fire or a cooking pot in the ten years I had lived the life of a begging monk, but I was too shy to admit my inability to cook, and I cut my finger with a knife, burnt the food and pot, depriving the Ashramites of their proper breakfast. I could see signs of discontent on some of their faces, and I felt extremely ashamed, but Dwarko said to me "You will also prepare lunch, but this time I will be with you to help."

Dwarko taught me how to cook. Learning how to cook was an agonisingly slow process, but gradually I learnt how to mix and make dough of wholemeal wheat flour to make chappatis, bread and pourris, and I cooked rice and vegetables and curry. Dwarko also taught me how to spin. I liked the beautiful musical sound of spinning, which made meditation easier. After six months I had made enough thread to make my own shirt and *dhoti* (a long piece of material used as trousers). I got rid of all those machine-made clothes and felt happy to have my own hand-spun clothes on my body.

During the morning I joined the eight other Ashram members in cleaning the buildings, and went to dig land to make a garden. For the first time in my life, I experienced the weight of a pick-axe and spade. About four acres of unproductive land had been donated to Vinoba for the purpose of starting the Ashram. Vinoba suggested that the main work of this Ashram should be "to find a synthesis between the intellectual and the manual, between the head and the hands, between contemplation and action, and between science and spirituality."

In order to achieve this integrated way of life, the day was divided into two parts. Before noon was devoted to manual work — digging, planting, spinning, weaving, etc. All the Ashram members were required to spend at least four hours doing these tasks. We were to earn our livelihood by working with our hands, thereby satisfying our physical needs. The afternoons were devoted to more personalised activites — whether it was writing poetry, painting, music, community work, political and social action — anything could be done according to the members' personal interests.

In the afternoon Dwarko said, "When you were a monk you were using your mind in meditation but never your hands to produce things. Now you must aim at integration of mind and body, hand and head, serving mother earth, working on the land is the path to spiritual enlightenment. You should live by three mantras cooking, digging and spinning."

In the ashram itself, I wasn't using money at all. Only when I had to go into the town and use a bus or a train did the ashram give me a little money. My total living expenditure could not exceed Rupees 30 (£2 at that time) per month. If I needed medicine, we grew some medicinal plants and roots. The emphasis was on prevention rather than cure.

Slowly, as weeks and months passed, I discovered that Ashram work was not only to dig land, cook food, and spin clothes. The Ashram was a centre for a large number of workers engaged in the area to bring about an equitable distribution of land. As long as land was not available to those who lived by it, as long as landless labourers were exploited by a few rich landlords and money-lenders, a cosy, self-sufficient, introverted Ashram life could not be a right way of living. Therefore, most of us spent a lot of time and energy to help the land for the people, Bhoodan movement.

Dwarko wrote a letter to Vinoba, explaining that I was now living in the Ashram. Vinoba answered at once saying that he was very happy that an ex-monk had come to join the Ashram and that after I had some experience he would like to see me. When my guru heard that Vinoba had accepted me, he was angry and got the chief minister of Rajasthan to write to Vinoba, saying that if Vinoba went on doing this sort of thing there would be no monks left in the order. Vinoba laughed and said "Let all the monks come and join the ashrams." I wrote a letter to Vinoba thanking him, and he wrote back saying that my name, *Bhairav*, sounded violent and that god Shiva who has many aspects and faces takes on the name 'Bhairav' when he is angry and destructive. Since I had started a new life I should be renamed. Vinoba suggested 'Satish', which means 'holder of truth'. So I changed my name to 'Satish' and adopted 'Kumar' as a second name because it does not imply caste as my family name had done.

I was living in a small mud hut in the Ashram with a wooden couch near the window on which I used to sleep. One afternoon I looked out of the window and saw a young Tibetan lama sitting on my verandah meditating. He was wearing a robe of deep brown, his head was shaven. I was spinning. He didn't speak, but closed his eyes and sat silently. It was like being in the company of a plant. After a while he began chanting some Tibetan mantras. I watched him, then I too closed my eyes and meditated with the sound. I offered him a raw sugar and lemon drink which he accepted without speaking. And then he went. He came often. Sometimes I followed him to the temple and the banyan tree under which Buddha had sat.

Ambadas was one of the more eccentric members of the Ashram. Vinoba had assigned to him the duty of keeping the Ashram and the village of Bodh Gaya clean. Every morning after breakfast he would put his enormous broom on his shoulder. Sometimes he would smilingly call to me "Hello Satish, let's go and sweep the streets of Bodh Gaya." and I would go with him. If he found much rubbish outside a house he would knock on the door and speak in a gentle voice. "My brothers and sisters, please don't make the street a dustbin." If he found excrement he would say "Streets are not toilets, please can you dig a hole and put your excrement in the hole and cover it with earth so that it can return to earth and not cause disease. Excrement left open in the air brings ill health and ill luck but buried under the earth it brings good fortune and fertility." Often he would say "The broom is my only friend." When we came back we would go to the well and pull out buckets of water and he would always scrub himself thoroughly with Lifebuoy soap. Then he would go back to his room and for the rest of the day he would do very little.

Ambadas was celibate from his childhood as indeed was Dwarko and our master himself, Vinoba. Ambadas had vowed to Vinoba that he would pursue a celibate life for ever. One day he disappeared. We went out looking for him and people from the village came to ask what had happened because he had never missed a single day's work. Later we found a letter among his clothes saying "I have decided to offer myself to the mother river and let her take me in her arms and absorb me in herself." Someone had seen him walking towards the river near the ashram but we never discovered his body — the river flowed very fast and he must have been swept quickly away.

I was sent for two months to the town of Gaya, to a craft school, to learn spinning with the Ambar wheel which has four spindles. I was given a hundred rupees to live on for the two months.

The town was on one side of the river and the craft school on the other. On the town side of the bridge, there was a narrow street. This street always blossomed in the evening. It was full of the sound of music and the air was heavy with the sweet smell of perfume. Here lived the women dancers and singers of the town. The atmosphere was gay and relaxed. Men wandered through in their light evening dress chewing betel leaves and buying jasmin garlands for their ladies. As I walked through, I looked up at a young woman, sitting on a balcony, decorated with red and blue lights. We caught each other's eyes and she smiled at me invitingly. Her lips were red with lipstick and betel leaves, her cheeks were rouged and her eyes darkened with Kajal. Her hair hung loose and she wore a red sari with a golden border. Her breasts were round and youthful.

I was with my craft teacher. I asked him if we could go to her. I was a little afraid. He agreed and both of us went upstairs to this young woman. She had two rooms, a sitting-room for talking and drinking and a bedroom. She came to me and put her arm on my shoulder, and stroked my hair. She kissed me. My body started shaking and shivering. I thought of being naked with her in the bedroom, lying beside her body. She pulled me towards her. I was frightened. I said "I have been a monk and have never been with a woman but I feel drawn to you." She said "You are young and it is quite natural that you feel attracted to me. Come here." I said "I want to talk to you, tell me about yourself." She said, "At the time of the partition of India my father, mother and many of my family were killed. I was left alone. I couldn't find a job or anywhere to live. People suggested that since I was a Muslim I should go to Pakistan, but I didn't know anyone there and I was too frightened to go. Then I met an agent and he introduced me to an elderly woman who taught me singing, dancing and making people happy."

I was more and more terrified of making love to a woman for the first time. I got up to go.

She asked, "Why are you going? Will you come again?"

"Yes, I will."

She said, "Come again, I like you. If you want, we can go to the cinema together."

I couldn't answer her. I gave her ten rupees and left.

I finished my course at Gaya and went back to the Ashram.

When Vinoba had been in the area of Bodh Gaya, he had persuaded many landlords and temple trustees to give land for distribution among the landless. A small amount of infertile land had been donated for the seventy-five landless untouchable families of Shekhwara. A meeting of the landlords and landless was organised to get better and more land for distribution. I gave a speech, the landlords looked bored, having heard the preaching of Vinoba workers many times before. They got up to leave. The *harijans* (untouchables) clustered round like shadows – not moving, not speaking. "I will not leave the village", I told them, "Until we have spoken to every landlord." No one responded no one spoke. Their eyes were bloodshot with weariness, their bodies and limbs taut with lack of nourishment. Upon these people lay generations of suffering – the cruelty of nature which gave them a searing sun and no water; conditions which bred smallpox, malaria and dysentery, and above all exploitation. They had been flogged and whipped and robbed of mind, these lowest of the low, the landless *harijans*, (the children of god – a name given by Gandhi). All that they produced, even their children, went to the cities as coolies. They lived without hope and there was no one to speak for them. They were forgotten people.

Most of the land around Shekhwara was owned by the Hindu temple in Bodh Gaya and was managed by an agent. One day at harvest-time I was visited by a young *harijan.* He crouched in the doorway, anxious and unsure what to do. I asked him to come in and sit down. He was hesitant.

"I'm a poor man, not worthy to sit with you."

"I'm a man and you're a man", I said.

"I'm poor. I was born in poverty and I will die in poverty."

I replied, "Poverty is not something ordained by God. Poverty is because you accept the exploitation of yourself. It's your right to live as a human being."

He sat down. He had been given two acres of land, but was as poor as before because he had no bullocks to plough with. He had a wife and two children to feed, so he had come to ask for help. Like the other *harijans* in the village, he was forced to work as a labourer on the temple land for only four pounds of rice a day. I went with him to the fields. The landless were all gathered there. At first they were reserved, then the complaints started to flow. A landlord who had given land had taken it back. Someone said that his homestead was on the temple land and they were asking him to leave. Another said that he had six children and four adults at home but the temple only allowed one person to work from each home. We talked for several hours. Clearly these people were ready to act, but the feeling of inferiority and helplessness was so deeply rooted that they felt incapable of doing anything alone. I suggested that we should go to talk to the agent of the temple who lived in Shekhwara.

As we drew near the agent's house, I could feel the *harijans'* sense of fear and apprehension. They walked slower and slower, looking on the ground. "We shall strike", I shouted in an effort to revive their spirits. They shouted in response, "Rich give land — poor give labour." By the time we reached the agent's house we had managed to create an atmosphere of confidence and strength. In the courtyard sheaves of paddy were stacked high and a team of bullocks were shuffling round and round on the threshing floor. The agent was eating his lunch. I could see his back through the doorway. He was a large man. I told him that we had come to protest about wages. He nodded curtly and continued eating. When he came out to join us, there was a hush.

Suddenly a young *harijan* jumped up boldly. "The land which now belongs to the temple once belonged to the village. We are very poor, but you take away all the grain and we don't see any of it. You stand over us from seven in the morning till three in the afternoon. We have decided to strike until you pay us more."

The crowd murmured. They were excited now. The agent shouted that he would hire labourers from other villages to harvest the land. He glared at me angrily.

"If the villagers had come to complain on their own without you Vinoba workers, I might have conceded. But you stir up trouble. You don't know these people as I do. They're lazy, good-for-nothing bastards. If they had a day's supply of food at home, they wouldn't work. They cheat and steal. Anyway, what do you think they do with their own land? Giving them land is like throwing gold onto the garbage heap."

I replied, "It's amazing the *harijans* have put up with these conditions for so long."

The agent said, "Of course they're always grumbling. You've just given them an excuse."

We persuaded the labourers from nearby villages not to work on the temple land, so the harvest went uncut, the grain began to rot. Then the agent came to talk to the village assembly and agreed to double the *harijans'* wage to eight pounds of rice per day.

I was invited to a marriage in a *harijan* family. I learned that the father had to take a ton of grain from the Hindu temple which was his landlord to provide the food for the marriage feast. As was the custom he must feed all his caste folk. Since he had nothing, he had no means of paying for the grain except by bonding his son to the landlord for the rest of the son's life. For the son it would be a double marriage – to his wife and to life-long slavery to the landlord. I tried to persuade the father to have a small party, but the father had been bonded in the same way, and he thought that if his son wasn't married in the traditional manner he wouldn't have respect in the village. I suggested, "Let every *harijan* family contribute a pound of grain to make the feast." But the father said, "How can I ask them to bring their food to my feast?" I said, "If the bonding of your son is part of the price of the marriage feast then I will not come to the marriage." He was sorry but he wouldn't act otherwise.

The other ashramites and I started a school for the village children. Out of the hundreds of children of the village only ten or twelve came and even these irregularly. I went to the *harijans* to persuade them to send their children to school. They said their children were looking after the cows, looking after the fields, minding the babies. "What good is school for them? We are untouchables, we sweep the streets, clean the toilets and work as labourers. We have no use for reading and writing."

The land of the *harijans* was barren because there was no means of irrigation. We started to build a well. The villagers gave their labour as a gift one day a week and a Vinoba admirer in Gaya gave the bricks and cement to build it. This was typical of how things were organised by the Ashram: everything was based on *dan* gift, *Bhoodan* (land gift), *Shramdan* (gift of labour), *Sampattidan* (gift of wealth), *Sadhandan* (gift of tools), *Budhidan* (gift of knowledge).

I went everyday at sunrise. There were about ten of us digging and five women carrying the earth. As we dug we left a spiral of earthen steps up which the women carried the basketsful of earth on their heads. Sometimes we had thirty or forty of us labouring and then we would stand in a line from the digging point to the point where the earth was to be thrown. We would not move but pass the baskets of earth along the line from hand to hand. When we went deeper we erected a pulley to take the earth up. People came from other villages, students came from the College in Gaya, to give their labour.

When the first bubble of water came we broke coconuts and offered them to God Shiva. "The water is the gift of the gods," people exclaimed. We distributed pieces of coconut with a lump of raw sugar to everyone present. When the village bricklayer completed the well another Vinoba admirer in Gaya made a gift of four pairs of bullocks with ploughs to be owned and worked collectively by the *harijans*. Soon the landscape was transformed. The *harijans* grew wheat in the spring and summer, rice in the monsoon rains, and vegetables, sugar and tobacco for their home use. Of course seventy acres of land with one well shared among seventy-five families did not make them wealthy but it made a small improvement in their material lives and a great increase in their self-confidence.

When I was digging the well, one of the women who came every day was Sita, the daughter of a *harijan*. I would dig, putting soil into a basket. When it was full, Sita came and stood close to me and I would lift the basket onto her head. How could I not notice her beautiful face, her black eyes, her dark skin and firm breasts through the thin tattered sari she wore? She walked fast up the steps out of the well to throw the earth so that she could stand beside me, waiting while I filled the next basket. We laughed and talked for those two months. Afterwards I used to see her occasionally and I always felt attracted to her. One day I asked Wasudev, a local supporter of our work, who employed Sita's father, if he thought it possible for me to marry Sita. He said 'A high caste man like you marrying an untouchable, an outcast! Such a thing has not been heard of in this village." I said "If I am ready for it, then it is up to me. Moreover breaking of caste barriers is an important part of my beliefs." Wasudev said "I doubt if Sita's father would agree to it." I said "Will you do me this favour? Will you be my messenger and ask him on my behalf?"

Next day Wasudev came with Sita's father, Hari. Hari looked reserved but cheerful. He wore a white turban and a silver earring in one ear, and carried a stick in his hand. He was relatively well off among his caste folk. He had a large family and so had been given two acres of *Bhoodan* (gift) land. His wife worked on road construction, and one of

Vinoba Bhave

his sons worked in Gaya so they were an enterprising family. I gave Wasudev and Hari some sherbet. Then Hari opened his mind and said "I am very honoured to hear that you wish to marry my daughter but sir, please do not make me break the customs carefully preserved from our forefathers. If by some temptation we break the custom once then nobody knows where it will end. Therefore I pray you not to entertain this idea any further." I said, "Hari, you are a wise man but you know that the tradition of untouchability has kept you and your people down. Will you not let us make a hole in this inhuman barrier?" Hari said, "We are very grateful to you and your leader Vinoba for the concern you have shown for us. If we can have land, jobs and houses then the caste barrier is no problem to us. We must follow our *dharmas*. You will find many young attractive women within your own caste who will be very happy to marry you. And as for Sita it is my duty to find her a suitable husband within my caste." I pursued it no further.

The followers of Vinoba were to meet together in the South, in Kerala. I had been living the Ashram life for about three years and here was an opportunity to get away and to meet Vinoba himself — the absent master of the Ashram.

I left the Ashram on a four day journey by train, through Calcutta and Madras. I arrived in the town of Kalari where the conference was to be held. A whole new tent city to accommodate ten thousand people had been erected there. People were arriving from every corner of India but Vinoba was still two days walk away. So I took a local bus to the village where he was.

When I arrived there was an atmosphere of a large number of people on the move. Mahadevi, who had been with Vinoba for thirty years and looked after his health, took me to him. He was sitting in a small hut on a couch, naked above the waist, wearing a simple linen cloth from his waist to his knees. On his head was his distinctive green peaked cap with earflaps tied under his chin. Many people were gathered round him, and he was reading. Vinoba greeted me and said "Tomorrow morning at four a.m. we start our march from this village to the next. Come and walk with me and we can talk."

Next morning Vinoba started out while it was still dark with someone walking in front of him with a lantern. A few minutes later he enquired where I was, but I was still sleeping. When I awoke I managed to catch the jeep which carried the sleeping rolls and luggage for the group. The driver took me to Vinoba.

Vinoba said, "This is the best part of the day to talk together. We have open skies, woods and mountains and fresh air. This is the time for fresh thoughts to come."

There were about thirty people walking. Many villagers lined the way to receive *darshan* from Vinoba. Women stood with decorated earthen water pitchers on their heads. Over the mouths of the pitchers were banana leaves held in place by coconuts — a sign of welcome. Occasionally Vinoba responded by bowing his head and putting both hands together touching his forehead.

Vinoba said, "By leaving the monk's life, you may find a real monk in you. Exclusive spirituality is not spiritual. And remember — as you did not get stuck in the monk life, don't get stuck in anything else. Keep flowing."

At dawn Vinoba sat on a hill and we gathered round him. He spoke on a passage from the Upanishads, and we sat in meditation and chanted the thousand names of Vishnu.

Vinoba said, "*Gramdan* (village cooperative) is different from the concept of socialism. We don't want to take power from the government. We want to bring the realisation of their power to the people. Then they will withdraw their support from existing governments and become their own government. If I were to enter politics directly, would it be possible for me to walk as I do today, a free man, with nothing to hinder me from speaking the truth as I see it? I should no longer feel the inward spiritual strength which I experience now. I could no longer roar like a lion. Politics and service do not go together; authority and power are not conducive to service. My aim is to build up a new kind of politics and in order to do so, I keep myself aloof from the old kind. This is politics of the people, as opposed to the politics of the power state."

When we arrived in the village there was an atmosphere of festivity, people greeted us with drums and flutes. We passed under bamboo archways laden with leaves, fruits and flowers. Banners proclaimed, 'Long live Vinoba, long live Gandhi.' In the village square Vinoba spoke, "My plea — that every son of the soil has a right to Mother Earth — is not my own. The Vedas have proclaimed it. No brother should prevent his brother from serving his mother earth . . . Land, like air, sun or water, is a free gift of God and what I am looking for, on behalf of the landless is no more than justice. Though my own stomach is very small, that of the poor is very big. Therefore I demand fifty million acres of land. If there are five sons in your family, consider me the sixth. I claim one sixth of the total cultivable land in the country for the poor. India is a country of God-intoxicated people. I believe that India can and should evolve a new type of revolution, based purely on love."

A landlord owning three hundred acres came and offered one acre of land. Vinoba said, "If I had been asking for a donation to erect a temple, I would be satisfied with your one acre, but I ask for land as a right of the poor and so I must refuse your offering." Then the man offered thirty acres and Vinoba accepted.

After two days walking, we arrived at Kalari. At the conference in Kalari Vinoba spoke to the gathered mass of his followers, "1957 must be made the year of total revolution. The land must be distributed among the people. There is a feeling in the air that some change is imminent. This change cannot come about by mere charitable work. We must initiate an act of aggressive love. I pledge that I will continue my walking pilgrimage until village self-government is achieved.

He said: "We have been trying to achieve a change of heart in the landlords by persuading them to see the problem in the villages as a 'land problem' and to solve it by getting them to make voluntary donations of some of their land. But the donated land is only a small fraction of the land of the village; the major part is still owned by a few rich landlords. The responsibility and problems of distributing the land is too vast for us. We must persuade the landlords that instead of merely donating a part of their land, they should transfer the ownership of all their land to the village community. Our new vision is to create villages with communal ownership of land.

He continued, "We are engaged in a People's Revolution. We must be supported by the people. It is not right for us to live off the interest of the Gandhi Memorial Fund. We must cut all ties with centralised financial aid and any bureaucratic organisational set-up. We should express in our lives and work the ideas of non-violent revolution . . . Let us go directly to the people and receive support from them. All the supporters of non-violent revolution – those who made a gift of land, those who received land and those who accepted non-violence as a means of social change – should keep a pot in their house, 'a *sarvodaya* pot', and a handful of grain should be taken by a child of the household

65

and put into this pot once every day. The grain collected in this way will provide our livelihood."

The conference proved to be a turning point for the Land Movement. One was Vinoba's pledge that he would not stop walking until the land problem was solved. Secondly the workers ceased to rely on centralised funds and made themselves dependent on support from the grass roots. Thirdly everybody reaffirmed their commitment to a total revolution to establish village self-government and village ownership of land. After three days of deliberations people dispersed. I went to Mahadevi and asked her if I could walk with Vinoba for a while. She accepted me as a member of Vinoba's marching party.

As Vinoba moved from village to village, there was an atmosphere of festivity and enthusiasm. He inspired the people and thousands came to greet him. Then when he spoke, people took the first step towards revolution, signing papers donating land to the village. He spoke in the language of the common people and this simplicity was one of the keys of his success.

It was miraculous that one man like Vinoba with his small army of volunteers could walk round the country and by his moral and spiritual authority be able to collect millions of acres of land for distribution among the poor and thousands of villages pledged to Gramdan.

While I was walking with Vinoba I learnt about Gandhi. Most of the people with Vinoba had either seen or lived with Gandhi. Gandhi's consciousness touched my consciousness. Vinoba's programme for a new society — a communitarian society without castes, injustices and eventually without the state was based on Gandhi's ideas.

I learnt about non-violence — that non-violence is not silence, not passivity, that non-violence is not merely not hitting or hurting physically or abusing someone with words, but it is a total relationship with the universe. This was a different concept of non-violence to the one I had learnt as a monk. Then I had not learnt to relate non-violence to other people; it was much more a personal rule rather than a right way of living with others. Now I understood that any kind of exploitation was violence. This Gandhian tradition of non-violence is referred to as walking with two legs. One leg is constructing the alternative society, the other leg is using non-cooperation to resist the

obstructions to change. I thought that Vinoba and the Gramdan movement were only walking on one leg, trying to create the alternative
society without challenging the power structure that was protecting
the old society. It seemed to me that Vinoba should launch a radical
civil disobedience campaign to force the landlords to adopt the principle
of collectivisation of land and to force the government to change the
laws of private ownership. Then the movement could get the momentum
necessary for the total revolution which Vinoba was calling for. *Gramdan*
(village self-government) was preparing for revolution, creating consciousness about property relationships and decentralisation of power
but it was not the revolution.

When I talked to Vinoba about it he said, "Gandhi used civil disobedience successfully against the British only because the British
government was not an elected government but an imposed authority.
The situation is different now. We are living in a democratic set-up. The
people have elected the government. If we want a change in government
we should tell the people who after all are the masters. Its no good
going to the government which is a servant of the people. My talk is to
create revolutionary consciousness in the minds of the people."

"But you should lead the people," I said.

Vinoba did not believe in leadership. "If you look for a leader in
me, you will be disappointed.", he said. "The time for political leadership is over. Now the people should become their own leaders." His
attitude was that to overcome landlordism, we should not resist the
landlords but assist them to act rightly. "Revolutionary feelings cannot
be developed in an atmosphere of opposition because opposition is
itself a form of violence. Opposition reduces the chances of a change of
heart. Instead of creating an atmosphere of sympathetic understanding,
it creates insecurity through which a man is drawn to defend himself
just at the point when he should be taking a new impartial look at
society."

He continued, "Take the example of a house. You want to enter
this house, but it has high walls around it. You go to the wall and fight
to get past it. You cannot. What happens? Your head is broken. But if
you find a small door, you can get into the house and go wherever you
want. But you have to find the door. Like that, when I meet a landlord
he has many faults and shortcomings, and his egotism is like a wall. But
he has a little door. If you are prepared to find this door, it means you

have risen above your own egotism and you can enter his life. Don't worry about his faults, only try to find the door. I am in search of that little door in every capitalist and landlord. If sometimes I cannot find the door it is my fault, my fault that I am banging my head against his shortcomings."

Vinoba himself had no ambitions. For him life was a search for knowledge of god. He saw the problem of India not as a political or economic problem but as a spiritual problem. He always said our tantra (technique) is Gramdan and our mantra is '*Jai Jagat*' (the unity of the universe). So Vinoba went on walking. "If the landlords, the capitalists and the exploiters are not converted today, they will be converted tomorrow. I will not stop until the whole nation is converted into village republics."

After three months of walking with Vinoba I returned to the Ashram. Taking up Vinoba's advice meant the end of the city-based, centrally-funded organisation of the movement. Those who felt they couldn't face life without a fixed monthly salary joined the establishment of Gandhian institutions in the cities. Others accepted the challenge of living either by the *Sarvodaya* pot or by their own manual labour. A group of sixty people from different Ashrams decided to live not in a fixed Ashram but as an 'Ashram on the March', with Khadigram Ashram as the base.

There was a bullock cart loaded with literature, clothes and other luggage and a microphone for making revolutionary propaganda. A small group would go to make advance publicity followed by the main group which would arrive at the village at breakfast time. People would invite the marchers to their houses for breakfast. After eating everyone would go with the people to wherever they were working, and join in their work. In the evening an open meeting would be held, encouraging the villagers to unite to form *gramdan* (a village community). If the response was good the marchers would stay for one or two days more to get the whole village to sign declarations of *Gramdan*. Sometimes a few of the group would remain for a longer period to give further advice and to consolidate the work. On average two in ten villages agreed to form a village commune.

My main responsibility was to be the line of communication between the people on the march and Khadigram Ashram. At Khadigram lived the families of the marchers as well as the minimum workforce to look after the animals and fields, and keep the craft workshops running. The Ashram accommodated about 200 people and was almost self-sufficient with 50 acres of paddy fields and a reservoir for irrigation. Married couples lived in family quarters with their children, bachelors lived in two room huts. All the houses were made of bamboo structure with walls plastered with mud and thatched roofs. The land, workshops and tools were run and owned collectively. It was an experiment in the combination of family and community. But basically the daily routine and lifestyle was the same as in the Ashram at Bodh Gaya, only here it was on a much larger scale. I spent half my time here and half my time with the people on the march.

One of the marchers was Kranti – a girl with a round face, dark eyes and long hair. I wanted to talk to her, but I was shy. On the march there was a strict separation between the men and women. When we arrived in a village, the women would go to one place and the men to another.

One day I came from the ashram bringing the post for the marchers and one of the letters was for Kranti. I kept it in my pocket. But as soon as she saw me coming she asked me if there was a letter for her.

I said, "Yes, there is."

She told me she was expecting a letter from her father.

I joked, "But you are a revolutionary, even your name Kranti means revolution. You should not keep too much contact with your father!"

She said, "I have come to see if you lot are revolutionaries or not". She laughed.

It was the day of *Holi* the spring festival of colours. People in the village were wildly throwing colours on each other. In order to escape the colour madness we all went to a waterfall in the mountains, walking through a forest. The trees were tall, the mountains steep and the footpath very narrow. I wanted to walk with Kranti, but she was with another girl. I was walking just in front of them, then stopped. To get past me, Kranti stepped off the path and a large thorn got tangled in her sari. I bent down to remove the thorn, taking as long as I could about it, and the other girl went on. Kranti and I walked together, almost out of sight of the others. Kranti told me that her father's letter urged her to come home immediately – one of her relatives was very ill. She wanted to leave that evening for Khadigram and we agreed to go together.

When we returned from the mountains the colour war was still going on. We could no longer remain aloof. I put many colours in a squirter and chased Kranti. I caught up with her and squirted colours on her beautiful cream and red sari and pasted her face with red powder and she did the same to me. In the evening we left the marchers. The bullock cart took us to a railway station. Although we were only about fifty miles away from Khadigram there was no direct train and we had to change twice and wait for connections. I had not imagined that I would be with Kranti like this. We had some milk and toast and bananas at the railway restaurant. I asked her to tell me about her family.

She said, "I have two sisters and a brother. My father is a professor of a college in a town in the foothills of the Himalayas. He grows herbs and eats natural good, mostly raw food. His passion in life is nature cure. When his students and friends are ill he treats them with water, mud poultices, sunbathing and fasting."

"Will you go to the same college where your father is?"

She said "I don't want to go to college, I would like to learn how to look after young children and start a centre for the care of young children, like a Kindergarten."

In the train we were sitting close to each other. She was tired and she fell asleep. I asked her to lie down and put her head on my knees and she did. I kept looking at her. Her face was serene and calm. We arrived at Khadigram in the early morning. The following day she left for her home but although physically she was gone my mind was full of her, every second I thought of her. Next day I sat down and wrote her a letter.

Dear Kranti, I hope you have arrived safely, You may be aware of it that you have pierced somebody's heart. Since you left I have not been able to do anything or think anything but you. The images of the day of Holi festival keep flashing across my eyes like a film. When are you coming back? I can't bear to be without you. I have fallen in love with you. Yours with love, Satish.

Kranti did not reply to my letter. I kept waiting for some word from her like a child. After three weeks Kranti returned to Khadigram. I asked her "Why didn't you answer my letter?" Kranti said "I was not surprised to get your letter but I didn't think that you should be encouraged. My father has been pressing me to get married. But I have no wish to marry. I don't want to marry, ever. Therefore I didn't want to reply to your letter. If I did, the next thing I would hear is a proposal to marry which I don't want. I asked "Why don't you want to marry?" She said, "For a women, marriage means a life of domesticity, cooking, looking after husband, cleaning the house, caring for the children. I want to be free from all this. So if you're falling in love means marriage then forget about it. My love for you is platonic. Love is like the ocean, you cannot put it in the bucket of marriage."

Weeks passed. We talked, worked together in the fields, went to the march and our friendship grew. Krishnaraj, one of the senior members of the Ashram, called me to him. He said, "Satish, I want to talk to you about a serious matter. Your friendship with Kranti is causing concern in the Ashram. If you and Kranti want I will write to her father and see if it is possible to arrange a marriage between you but it is not right in the discipline of the Ashram that two young unmarried people should be seen together so much." I said "Kranti does not want to marry and our relationship is platonic, a pure love untouched by physical sexuality." Krishnaraj said "I am sorry, but this must stop. This cannot be allowed. If you both feel strongly for each other I am afraid one of you will have to leave the Ashram. We cannot let the atmosphere of the Ashram be filled with gossip and speculation. The life we live here must be disciplined."

I was taken aback by his words. I could not live in Khadigram and not meet Kranti. Even if I forced myself not to meet Kranti I could not stop thinking of her. So I decided that the best course for me was to leave Khadigram. That evening I told Kranti what Krishnaraj had said. She was very upset. She urged me not to leave. She said, "Even if we don't meet and talk to each other at least we can see each other if you are here, but if you go when will we ever see each other?"
I said, "If I stay we will both be miserable. If we are in the Ashram we have to accept the rules, and I can't accept them so I must move on. I have decided to go to Benares. You must come to meet me there."

Benares

Benares was a mysterious city. The more I lived in it, the more I liked it. It was a city without speed. I lived in a house in a narrow alley where only pedestrians and cows were able to wander. In this old city I felt all around me a sense of timelessness. Life seemed as it might have been a thousand years ago. In every street there were many things quietly happening. There were astrologers of great learning, teachers, musicians and beggars, but behind the mask of a beggar might be a great sadhu (spiritual seeker).

Benares was full of dirt and filth, but the dirt was like compost for beautiful people. Near the house where I lived was a brahmin, a teacher of sanskrit. I used to watch him every day through my window. He imparted his knowledge to his students in an intimate atmosphere. I watched him playing devotional ragas on his sitar and going to the Ganges every morning chanting Vedic verses (mantras). His students would come after bathing, with flowers in their hands. They worshipped Shiva lingam together, offering the flowers and burning incense. They sang aloud sanskrit verses, learnt by heart. They seemed like members of one family.

One day while I was talking to him I asked him how he earned his living? He looked at my face with surprise and I felt ashamed of my question. He said, "I never thought about it. It just comes." He told me that he had been living in this street for fifty years and had never left Benares in his whole life.

From time to time I had been writing articles and reports of the Ashram on the March and walking with Vinoba for the weekly Hindi language newspaper of the *Bhoodan* (land gift) movement, published from Benares. When I discovered that there was a vacancy for the deputy editor I went to see Siddaraj Dhadda, the editor. He had liked my reports and was very happy to employ me. This meant that I had an income and a place to live in the community house where all those who worked for the paper were living. The offices of the paper were on the ground floor and we lived in rooms above, sharing the community kitchen. We observed some of the practices of the Ashram — communal prayer early in the morning and one hours' spinning as our manual labour.

Kranti came to Benares and stayed in the community house. At dinner I asked her to meet me afterwards. I kept waiting for her in my room. When I heard any footsteps I thought it was her. Hours passed, the night passed, no sign of either sleep or Kranti. When we met at breakfast I gave her a poem. At lunch she gave me a slip of paper — "If the other people living in the building see me walking to your room it would create misunderstanding, but I will meet you at the Ganges at eight o'clock tonight."

The day became very long. I reached the appointed place almost an hour early. Kranti came exactly on time. It was a beautiful night. We hired a small boat and floated slowly to the other side of the river and sat on the shining sand under the moon.

"You wanted to speak to me. Why are you so silent?" Kranti asked.

I answered, "Perhaps I just wanted to be with you and say I love you."

Kranti said, "Are you sure that you love me? Because I see no connection between love and sex."

I said, "I don't think I can exclude sex from love.

Kranti said, "True oneness is above physical sex."

We lay all night on the sand.

Kranti said, "I don't want you to suffer because of me. Why don't you get married? I would like to help you find a wife, and once you're married all this gossip about our relationship will stop and our friendship can continue."

Next evening we met again and we went to drink *bhang*. (Cannabis and milk drink). We walked through various *bhang* shops, watching the sellers preparing it. In one of the shops there were pictures of Shiva, the god of *bhang*. We went in. There was a pleasant smell of joss-sticks. Two glasses of *bhang*, with almonds, milk and cream, were prepared and served. The taste was sweet, smooth and cool. Suddenly the whole shop disappeared and the street came into it. One street came in, disappeared, then another came. I saw a man enlarging his body to an enormous size so that the whole street was filled by him. His long hair was tied together on top of his head, his face was angry. He put on different bodies. He became my father dying. He became monk Kundan lying dead, surrounded with flowers, incense and peacock fans. In an instant he changed and became my guru. I was pursued by death. I started hitting my head to bring myself back to normal. Kranti called

74

a rickshaw and helped me into it. I tried to jump out but she held onto me. I cried out "Let me go. There's no home and no one is waiting for me there." She took me to the house. I lay down on the bed. She sat by me. She brought me some lemon to drink, stroked my hair and put a cool wet cloth on my head. I fell asleep.

Benares was the city of Shiva, in it there were many Shiva temples. I used to go to the Nepalese temple overlooking the Ganges where the walls were covered with erotic sculptures and carvings. The centre of the temple was a large Shiva lingam (Shiva penis statue) standing erect, coming out of the yoni (vagina) of Parvati the goddess. Above the lingam hung a clay pot from which drops of water fell onto the lingam, then trickled down into the yoni.

There was a man sitting beside the lingam on a deerskin. He was old with glaring eyes, silver-white long hair down to his hips, and a silver beard stained with the yellow of smoke. He was Babaji, the Keeper of the temple. I placed fruit and flowers at the statue and I sat beside Babaji in silence. I made the offering for many days.

One day Babaji asked me to fetch some water from the Ganges to fill up the clay pot above the lingam. The following day I found him cleaning the temple and asked if I could clean it. He put his hand gently on my head and gave me the broom.

One day he said, "Look at all these people coming here to see the temple. They see the external lines, but they have no understanding of them."

I asked what it was they did not understand.

He said, "It's too late in the day. You must come earlier."

"At six o'clock?"

"Six o'clock is devil's time. Four o'clock is the time of the Lord God. What can you understand by coming to me — you see only this old beard, a toothless face and a thin body? No need to come."

In the courtyard of the temple, there was a little hut. Overshadowing the hut was a large old banyan tree, and underneath the tree was a blanket on which Babaji slept. Here he did his yoga and meditation, first standing on his head then standing upright and completely still. Babaji told me, "I practise *Wam Marg* (left path). I worship Shiva the three-eyed god and his consort Shakti the source of all energy and

75

power. Conversation came slowly. Often he closed his eyes and went into his inner world. If I asked ten questions, Babaji would answer half a question. He would say, "It's not possible for me to tell you in words. I am seventy-seven. If you think I have achieved something, it has been by doing and experiencing."

Once after I had been asking questions, he didn't reply but took a thin piece of linen cloth four yards long, chewed then swallowed it all except for a small piece which he held in his hand. Then he slowly pulled it out and on the cloth were stains of blood and food. It had gone right through his stomach. Another time he put a piece of string in one nostril and pulled it out through his mouth.

Babaji said, "The Serpent power in our bodies is like the cobra. When the cobra is provoked, it is one of the wildest animals. It bites and you have no life. But it is hidden unless awakened. Through the tantra (secret technique) you awaken the power centres of the body, the seven *chakras* (wheels) and the *kundalini* (serpent power). The sexual union is the basis of all. Orgasm without ejaculation by sucking the sperm back into the body up the spine awakens the supreme energy of our consciousness. The centre above the brain opens like a lotus." Then the body becomes the true temple of god.

One morning Babaji said, "I don't think you are ready for this path. If you want to do Gramdan, do it. If you want to change the world, go away and change the world."

I was frightened. I could feel his power challenging me. I sat down beside him and said, "Please teach me something more."

He replied, "You need full commitment and total surrender which I don't see in you. Either come in or go away."

We sat in silence. I put my head on his feet. He understood that I was leaving. He didn't ask me to stay.

There was rioting in Assam between Bengalis and Assamis, and many were killed. Nehru, then prime minister, went to Vinoba who was walking in the northwest of India, and said to him, "Only your saintly message will calm people's emotions. Your presence in Assam can bring harmony to the riot torn communities." Vinoba decided to walk to the east to Assam but refused the offer to fly him there. He said, "In the modern world my words can reach Assam by radio and newspaper. My prayer and contemplation will have greater power than my physical presence there and my act of walking to Assam from here is a prayer in itself." On his way to Assam he came to Benares, which he himself knew well as a student. He found our city very dirty. People had been using the banks of the Ganges as public toilets and then washing themselves in the river, believing Mother Ganges had the power to purify everything. At a public meeting Vinoba urged people to build proper toilets. Then he said, "When I speak only my beard moves, but if we all take brushes we can move the filth away."

Next morning a group of us walked with Vinoba to the river holding brushes and wheeling dustcarts. By the time we had reached the river bank there were about a thousand people. The Mayor of Benares was there, the leading members of the Brahmin community, the professors of Benares University, none of whom would ever think of even touching a broom, were there carrying brooms. They were all photographed with Vinoba holding brooms, even if they did not help very much in the sweeping they created a good impression and the 'Clean Benares' campaign got off to a good start. Together we cleaned the Dashashwamedh ghat, the holiest of the holy steps going down to the river. Vinoba said "We should not let this enthusiasm die down. We should organise a group of young people who will go from door to door persuading people to take their part in the 'Clean Benares' campaign." I joined a group of volunteers. Each day we walked through the city street by street. We cleaned and swept as we went. We visited homes. In the evening we held public meetings and we were fed and looked after by the inhabitants of the streets.

While we were sweeping the streets and talking to people about the life and work of Gandhi and Vinoba some of our listeners were not slow to point out that a new Gandhian complex of buildings, which included the offices of the paper which I was editing, was being completed on the outskirts of the city at the cost of half a million rupees. This could not be considered an example of the simple living of the Gandhian kind. I agreed and wrote an article in a local newspaper, criticising the building of such expensive offices for ourselves rather than using the donated money in the villages. I also questioned the need to establish yet another organisation, the Gandhian Institute of Studies, which was to employ university graduates at high salaries to do research and translate Gandhian ideas into the language of the social sciences

77

with an obsession for charts, facts and statistics. This article brought me into direct conflict with the organisation. The deputy director of the Institute said to me, "How can we trust you if you express your disagreement in public like this?" I said "Whether I express myself in public or private the fact remains that we are wasting time and money in giving the Gandhian philosophy an academic face. If our movement is a people's movement it must speak the people's language not the language of academics."

For me this man, this institute and this building represented that wing of the Gandhian establishment which is career conscious, western suited, city orientated, intellectual, salary seeking, those who felt it necessary to do a public relations job on the movement to fit it to the urban, industrial twentieth century. They took the name of Gandhi but they were diametrically opposed to the simplicity of Gandhi. My opposition to the Institute and criticism of the smart new offices brought me the sack, though against the wishes of the editor, and in some ways it was a relief to me that I never moved in to those buildings I despised.

While I was working with Siddaraj Dhadda a close friend of his was looking for a husband for his daughter Lata. In the three years I'd known him Siddaraj had taken on a fatherly role towards me and he wanted to arrange my marriage. He wrote to his friend Suranaji proposing a marriage between Lata and me. As was the custom there was a lengthy exchange of letters giving life histories and photographs, and matching of horoscopes. Suranaji was a businessman and would have liked to have married his daughter to a businessman but all previous attempts to do so had failed. From her photo Lata looked very attractive, she was nineteen years old, she had been to school for ten years and was gentle and good mannered, able to cook and sew. Lata and I were to meet in the presence of her family before a final decision was taken.

Dhadda and I travelled five hundred miles to Hinganghat to see Lata and her family. They had a large three-storey house, the front of which was the family drapery shop. We sat in the shop on thick, large cushions on the floor. The whole family was there, the mother, the brother, the uncle and his son and a few close friends. Lata's brother served us with tea and sherbet and a big tray of sweets and savouries, pistachio and almond halva, gulab jamon, samosas etc. Apart from Lata's mother this was a male gathering. Women peeped through the curtained doorway at the back of the shop. After some time Lata came with a silver tray filled with betel leaf and nuts. She walked slowly, but appeared full of energy, her eyes were cast down, her sari covering her head revealed just a little of her black hair parted in the centre. The sari was orange with a red border and red blouse. Her bangles of silver and glass tinkled as she walked. Her face was round, her eyelashes edged her eyes with black, her fish shaped eyes. She offered the *pan* to me after which she sat shyly near me. We liked each other immediately. She was a fine looking woman. In a few minutes she was gone. There was no opportunity for conversation.

Coming back in the train Siddaraj said "Marriage is a way of performing your social and communal responsibility. It is your *dharma* to accept the love of woman and unite with her. Love does not come by accident or chance, you don't fall in it, you cultivate it. In my view Lata will be a good companion for you.

It was a long time before Lata's father wrote to me. I heard that he was trying to persuade Lata to marry some well-established young man, but Lata insisted that she would only marry 'the man from Benares'. Eventually the engagement ring was brought to me by Lata's brother, and I gave to him an engagement ring and Benares saris for Lata. The date for the marriage was fixed for two months later.

About fifty friends of mine, mostly those who worked with the Gramdan movement, came with me to attend the marriage. Lata's family had arranged for a Brahmin to perform the marriage ceremony. The family house was decorated with young banana trees in clay pots, forming arches and pathways. Silvery stars in red, green and blue hung from the windows. Coconuts entwined in ropes hung from the walls. Clay water pots painted in broad strokes stood on top of each other in corners. As we entered young girls sprinkled jasmin and rose and musk scent on the clothes of all the guests. Lata and I sat on silk cushions under a silk umbrella. The soles of her feet and the palms of her hands were intricately patterned with a red dye. Her face was powdered with glitter. Strings of jasmin flowers hung from her hair. She was wearing the traditional red sari with gold embroidery and jewellery on her body. Lata and I sat in the centre of the courtyard, Agni, the goddess of fire, blazed in front of us. She was the sacred witness to our union. Lata's hand was placed in mine and both our hands were bound together with a silk scarf. The Brahmin pronounced a mantra. A corner of Lata's sari was knotted to a corner of my shawl. The Brahmin pronounced another mantra. Thus tied together we walked seven times around the fire. Lata's uncle took her in his arms and carried her round me seven times. The Brahmin said "Satish Kumar, take Lata as your companion in the living of your life. Look at her, never see enough of her, cherish her with the eyes of love. Lata, love him well forever, walk with him as his wife and follow him like his own shadow forever. I marry you."

I put a garland of flowers on Lata's neck and she put one on mine. Flute and *shahanai* and drums played ceremonial music. Hundreds of people ate sweets and festive food and drank sherbets and milk shakes, and rose petal flavoured drinks, friends read poems giving us blessings. Next morning Lata was sent with me wrapped in a yellow sari. Her mother was crying and Lata was crying. Lata's brother accompanied us. When we arrived in Benares, we were received at the station by many friends. Lata was loaded with garlands. In comparison with her family home my flat was very small — no cupboards, and not much furniture. A friend of mine had decorated the flat with flowers and fruits. Lata's father had given us an eiderdown, blankets, pillows, clothes, cooking pots, plates, water jugs etc. I had almost nothing, Lata brought everything with her. In the evening her brother left and we were alone together for the first time. We unpacked, made the bed, arranged our new and shining possessions, laid the carpet and sat eating sweets but Lata spoke very little. I longed to embrace her, but she was afraid.

"Please don't come near me like this," she said.

I tried to persuade her.

She said, "I'm told it's very painful. I don't want it."

My friends had told me not to hurry and to let longing arise in her. She lay down on the mattress and covered her body and face. I lay beside her trying to think how to persuade her. It was dark. I drew back the cover slowly, opened the buttons of her blouse and removed her sari and petticoat. I found my way inside her. She gasped, then turned aside to sleep. I lay awake. It had just been a physical act without any contact or love. I felt guilty and disappointed.

That was how our married life started. From the beginning things went wrong. I had all kinds of ideas in my head about what kind of woman she should be and what she should do, but Lata didn't conform to any of them. Her mother had told her never to eat before her husband, so in the evening she would still be waiting for me, no matter how late. It took me some time to convince her to eat with me. Her parents were anxious to know how she was getting along and they wrote saying it was their custom to take their daughter back soon after marriage so that she wouldn't feel homesick. So Lata's brother arrived to take her home. After a month I went to fetch her again. This time she was more relaxed and happy, but I was still disappointed. Our relationship never was satisfactory sexually. She thought it was a moment when she had to give in, and I felt I had to take something she didn't want to give.

It wasn't easy financially either. The money from the weekly paper was barely enough to live on. I was always trying to reduce our needs, but Lata wasn't used to that way of life − she had lived all her life with her father who was relatively rich. Before if she wanted to buy shoes, go to the cinema or a restaurant she could always do so, now we couldn't afford it. As a result we quarrelled over money. I tried to explain to Lata my relationship to money. "We should stretch our legs only the length of our blanket, which means reducing our needs if that is what the situation demands. I feel if we follow money we will become its shadow. We try to catch it, but it always is beyond our grasp. I have never felt the desire to be rich. The cobra doesn't serve any master and birds do not work to produce food. Those who do not worry get their provision from the creator. He who has given a mouth will put food in it."

Lata argued, "Then you live off other people."

"I don't live "off" others. I receive maximum and give maximum. and I reduce my needs to the least."

Vinoba had started a new ashram in the south of India about ten miles from Bangalore, called Vishwaneedam which means 'The Nest of the World'. Swamiji, a disciple of Vinoba and head of the Ashram, was visiting Benares and looking for more people to come to live there. One of my friends, Prabhakar, was there. So after I was sacked from my weekly paper I decided Lata and I should go to Vishwaneedam.

We journeyed two thousand miles to the south. The Ashram was situated in the Nilgiri hills with many sandalwood trees, mango groves and beautiful lakes and land where we could grow our own food. Lata and I had our own room. There was a big community kitchen for all the members. The food was simple and without spices.

After we joined the ashram Lata realised she was pregnant. She told me it was the custom in her family for the daughter to return to her parents to have her first child. Her father wrote to me that he and Lata's mother would like her to come home and that he was sending her brother to take her. I was conscious that the conditions at the Ashram were not so convenient for the birth. Also Lata felt isolated being so far in the country — the people were not of her type and very few people spoke our language, Hindi. So I agreed and Lata went with her brother.

Cancelled from
Gladstone's Library

2 4 JUL 2024

GLADSTONE'S
LIBRARY

Wanderer

One afternoon I was having coffee with Prabhakar Menon in a cafe in Bangalore. Prabhakar and I had become close friends since living in the Ashram. He was just a year older than me. We had similar ideas, similar interests and similar tastes. He came from Kerala, in the deep south, but had learnt to speak Hindi, a language of North India, fluently. We were talking about the problem of nuclear disarmament. He had with him the Deccan Herald, an English language daily. He read out to me the news of Bertrand Russell's arrest in an anti-nuclear demonstration in London.

Russell had said "Today a handful of people in a few countries are vested with power to preside over the destiny of mankind. It is the duty of every common man to rise up and expose the intrigues of the big powers which may lead to the destruction of humanity . . ."

I thought — here is a man of ninety committing civil disobedience, what are we doing in India? What am I doing?

Suddenly Prabhakar had a brilliant thought, "Why don't we start a peace march to Moscow, Paris, London and Washington, the four nuclear capitals, and demonstrate physically our opposition to the nuclear nonsense.

It was a brainwave and I grasped it.

"We shall do it," I shouted and thumped the table with my fist.

Prabhakar was encouraged and happy at my sudden and total acceptance. "Do you think the two of us are enough for the job?"

"It's the job that matters, not the number."

Carried away by our enthusiasm we ordered more coffee. The decision had been made.

It was only a few months since I had got married. I was reluctant to tell Lata of my scheme when she needed all my affection and support. As I wavered, a whole month passed. I was grappling with world problems, but the problem of leaving my pregnant wife seemed to defy all solutions and left me helpless. So I wrote her a letter, telling her of my plan to walk from Delhi to Washington, justifying it with some idealistic phrases such as 'personal responsibility for the fate of the world', 'not wanting to be a passive onlooker while the world is rushing headlong into a suicidal arms' race', 'a voice crying in the wilderness'.

I told her I would take my final decision only after she gave her whole-hearted consent. The letter I received from Lata was a surprise. "Your undertaking is full of faith and courage. Had I not been pregnant I myself would have liked to accompany you on your peace pilgrimage. Please don't take any decision before the birth of our child. Being our first child it has some privilege over us, doesn't it?"

I went to see her. We talked about my plans. She suggested that with her mother and brother we should rent a house in Bangalore so that we could be together for the remainder of her pregnancy.

We rented a small house in the suburbs of the city and found a hospital. We all took care to give Lata an undisturbed pregnancy. During this time Lata and I had many discussions about the proposed walk and she agreed to it fully. Her brother had found a job in Bangalore and wanted to stay. Her mother too was very happy in the city, so they both agreed to stay and look after Lata and the baby until my return. The Gramdan organisation agreed to support the walk and pay me a bursary which was sent to Lata while I was away.

Swamiji said, "You are going to the world as emissaries of our Ashram."

On 22 April 1962 Lata gave birth to a baby girl in Bangalore Hospital. I was not allowed to be with her. I waited outside the delivery room. An hour after the birth I was allowed to see our infant. We called her Sadhana which means seeking. Lata's face was radiant, she had for-given me for that harsh and unwanted act of love on our first night together, nine months ago. With Lata's agreement Prabhakar and I fixed the date – to leave Bangalore on the 10th May for our world journey. My elation at being now free to go was tinged with sorrow and some reluctance to leave the newly born babe. Lata said, "Your baby will be in good care and I will look after her and be father as well as mother to her. She will remind me of you but also keep me company in my lonely times. Don't let it be said that a woman held you back from your adventure."

Lata was there with our baby daughter on the railway platform to say goodbye. She had brought some flowers for me, but there were tears in her eyes. I was silent.

First we went to see Vinoba to seek his blessings. Vinoba was still walking in Assam. When we arrived he greeted us with his familiar smile. He was already informed about our plans and started probing us about our journey, opening an atlas in front of him. He wanted to know which route we were taking, the preparations we had already made, the countries we were going to visit.

Next morning we joined him in his eternal walk. He put his right arm on my shoulder, his left arm on Prabhakar's shoulder and so we walked.

He asked, "How much money are you taking with you?"

We told him "Some business friends have agreed to bear some of our expenses and will arrange for foreign currency to be available for us in some of the countries we journey through. Vinoba became silent.

"Do we have your blessing, Vinoba?" I asked.

He remained silent for some moments longer then said quietly,

"It's a long journey. You'll need some protection. I want to give you two 'weapons' to protect you."

"How can non-violent people carry weapons?" I asked.

"Non-violent people carry non-violent weapons," Vinoba replied. "The first weapon is that you will remain vegetarian in all circumstances; the second is that you will carry no money, not a single penny."

"How can we live without money on such a long journey?" I asked.

Vinoba said, "You were a begging monk for nine years, how did you live without money? Because your pot was empty, you could fill it. Money is an obstacle to real contact with people. If you are tired after walking you will find a hotel to sleep in, you will find a restaurant to eat in and you will never meet people. But if you have no money you will be forced to speak to people and ask humbly for hospitality. Secondly, when you are offered hospitality you will say, "I'm sorry but I eat only vegetables." People will ask you why? Then you can tell them about your principles of non-violence and peace. This will open communication."

Prabhakar and I looked at each other. We were both convinced of Vinoba's 'weapons' and we promised him that we would do as he suggested. Vinoba said, "I am very happy. Go with courage and faith. The world will meet you with open arms, you will fulfill yourselves in this journey. I bless you. God bless you."

The sky was overclouded. Again and again we had to quicken our steps to keep up with Vinoba who was walking briskly along the zigzag path leading through the mountains. We felt as if he was teaching us how to walk. He asked again about our route. We told him that we

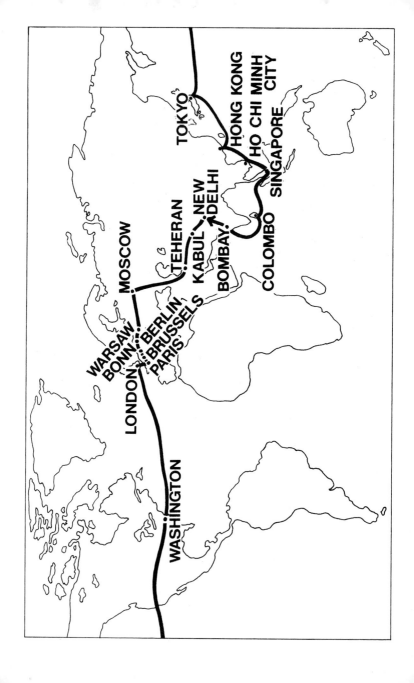

intended to travel through the Khyber pass, enter Afghanistan and cross over the Hindu Kush mountains and take the direct route to Tashkent and thence to Moscow. Vinoba said, "Although that route is the most direct it may not be the best for your purpose. In the Hindu Kush there are few passes open through the year and very few people live there. Also after Tashkent there will be long stretches of desert between villages and nowhere for you to stop for the night. Why not take the more populated route through northern Persia? The cultural links between India and Iran have been strengthened by many travellers over the centuries."

Once again he put his hands on our shoulders and silently looked at us with great love.

We left Vinoba and went by train to Delhi.

Earlier we had applied for our passports in Madras. The Madras passport authorities interpreted our walk as 'political' and forwarded our applications to the Foreign Affairs Ministry in Delhi. They told us we had to furnish a guarantee of twenty thousand rupees as security in the event of our needing repatriation. Who was going to bear this responsibility for us? At last a lawyer friend of mine, M. L. Jain in Calcutta presented the security. But in spite of completing all the necessary formalities, we were still without our passports. In the scorching heat of summer we did the rounds of the various departments of the Foreign Affairs Ministry. In the nightmarish world of government bureaucracy a passport was like a mirage, always beyond our reach. Finally we decided to abandon the wild goose chase for the passports and start our walk without them.

The clouds we had seen in Assam soon caught up with us. On 1 June they suddenly burst down in torrential rains. That day we went to Gandhi's grave. As we stood there in silence, a cool breeze started blowing, awakening in us a new sense of life. It was under hanging clouds that Vinoba had given us his blessings; and now standing before the grave we were once again enveloped by rain and clouds. I seemed to hear Gandhi's soft, almost caressing voice in the falling rain "Don't forget that the people are as generous as the clouds and their hearts can be as tender as the raindrops." Gandhi and Vinoba. Vinoba and Gandhi. Somehow their separate blessings mingled into a single sound – soothing our anxieties, filling our hearts with courage. We made the pledge: let people alone be the source of our sustenance, and let us never carry money during the course of our walk.

A newspaper published the news that peace-marchers were going on foot from Delhi to America to promote the cause of world peace, but they had with them neither passports nor money. There were questions in parliament as to why the government had failed to give us passports. Nehru, then prime minister, promised he would go into the question himself and just as we were nearing the Pakistan border, on 2 July, our passports were delivered to us. We had walked 370 miles in thirty-two days in the burning heat of June. Each day we had set off in the cool hours of dawn usually after a breakfast of mangos and milk. But for the first few days we suffered from bleeding blisters and acheing muscles.

Thirty-five men and women accompanied us on our last day in India to bid us farewell. We knew no one in Pakistan and everyone seemed anxious about what would happen to us when we entered. Women insisted we should carry some food with us in case we didn't get anything to eat there. They all thought of us as going to an enemy country. After all India and Pakistan had been in a state of war over Kashmir since 1947. We said that taking food with us meant that we distrusted the Pakistani people. Hearing this, a grandma placed her palms on our heads saying, "You're my sons. Do the best for the world . . .". On 3 July we crossed the Indian border.

Entering Pakistan where we had not one contact, to our intense surprise we were met by a young man who presented us with flowers. He said "When I read in my local newspaper that two travellers are coming with a message of peace and no money in their pockets, I decided to meet you and take you to my house, sixteen miles from here in Lahore . I have been waiting for you for hours. Please get in my car and be my guest." We said "How kind you are. We would love to come to your house but not in your car. Give us your address and we should reach you by walking towards evening." The young man seemed unconvinced. He said, "You might find someone else on the way and I might never get the chance of being your host. So come with me now, and make an exception." We said, "We promise to come and stay with you." He thought for a moment and said "I can only accept your promise if you give me your rucksacks as a guarantee that you will at least come to collect your baggage." We laughed and gave him our rucksacks.

A few miles later another man rushed out into the road and stopped us. He said, "Your host for tonight has told me all about you. I have prepared your lunch. Please come and rest and eat lunch with me." We were moved. We were hungry and thirsty. We went into the cool of his house. He had prepared rice and salad and lentil soup but the main dish particularly cooked for us, as a special treat for his guests, was fish freshly caught from his pond. We were hesitant to say to him that we could not eat fish. However when we explained that we were vegetarian, he understood. As we approached Lahore, by the Shalamar Gardens we saw our host approaching. He said, "It is better that I walk with you so that you don't get lost in this huge and congested city," and indeed Lahore was huge and congested. The Rickshaws, the buggys, the cars, the buses, the pedestrians filled the narrow streets. We walked through Anar Kali Bazaar where life was in full swing. Men relaxed, walked along wearing freshly starched muslin shirts (kurta) and trousers and all with white embroidered muslin caps stiff with starch. Hundreds and hundreds of men clad in white packed the pavements. Against this white background stood out the black Borkas in silk or cotton of the women. The women were covered from head to toe, with only a small area of gauze as their contact point with the outside world. The unmarried young girls were the only ones to add colour to this black and white world. They wore skin tight trousers and shirts in gaudy colours of red, yellow, blue, purple, pink – you name it, they wore it, all gleaming in silk and satin. A thin nylon or chiffon scarf they threw over their hair as a token of feminine modesty on their provocatively dressed youthful bodies.

Our host guided us through this sea of humanity. He lived in an old house in a small lane. He insisted on our staying for more than one night, which was our plan. We met his friends, walked around the city, ate our fill of Lahore delicacies. And on the third day we bade him farewell.

It took twenty-six days to walk the distance of 327 miles across Pakistan. Whether it was a rickshaw driver, vegetable seller or farmer, whoever saw us on the road with placards on our front and rucksacks on our backs would stop for a moment to have a word with us. Everywhere people would ask to which community or religion we belonged.

To all such questions we replied, "We are human beings, first and last. Our religion is our faith in humanity — and there can be no religion greater than that. If we come as Indians, we will meet Pakistanis. If we come as Hindus, we will meet Christians or Muslims. If we come as socialists, we will meet capitalists. If we come as human beings, we meet human beings everywhere."

After walking almost two months, we found ourselves at the last frontier post of Pakistan — the Khyber Pass. The local authorities warned us that to walk from Delhi was alright but to go on foot through the tribal pass wasn't safe. We assured them that we came to 'observe, listen and love.' After some difficulty the government authorities in Peshawar agreed to let us go on the condition that we were accompanied by four armed guards. We walked over the winding roads of this mysterious land alongside the small, snaking river which constantly provided us with refreshing and thirst quenching, cool water. To the left and right of us mountains rose up steeply piercing the sky. Every now and then we met an army post guarding the frontier. The frontier through which so many invaders had come. Walking through this land of battles we murmured our *mantra* of peace in the presence of our armed guards who stayed with us for twenty-four hours. On our way we had frequent talks with the tribal people (Pathans) we met. "Much malicious propaganda is made against us," some of them told us. "Consequently we feel ignored and isolated. If a guest comes, God comes in him. We carry arms to protect our guests, even at the cost of our own lives."

After the Khyber Pass, we walked through the barren plains and high mountains of Afghanistan. When we were hungry we walked into gardens by the road and picked huge egg-shaped melons with yellow and green stripes. The taste, texture and flavour was such that we called them fruits of paradise. Both melons and grapes were abundant — even the donkeys were given them to eat. We feasted ourselves on almonds, pistachio nuts and hundreds of kinds of dried fruit which people gave us as we passed through mountain villages and nomad camps. In the evenings we went to the *kahva* (green tea) houses where there were handwoven, earthy coloured carpets and people sitting cross-legged, relaxed with round cushions behind their backs. When we asked if we could stay the night there, the response was always warm and generous, and we would be given cup after cup of tea with fresh home-baked bread.

In Kabul we stayed with an Indian businessman. He was very happy to see two of his countrymen on a journey of adventure. He equipped us with warm clothing, soap, toothpaste, and shoes. He provided us with enough stamps to write to everybody back home and to some contacts en route. We rested and wrote our travel stories to various papers.

Kabul appeared to us as the capital of glorious donkeys. They brought fruit, vegetables and nuts from the surrounding countryside and took back the consumer items of the city. They added their charm to the Kabul streets. A week's stay in the cool breezes of Kabul refreshed us and we moved on.

There were three roads to Herat. The northern road built by the Russians, the southern road built by the Americans and the traditional track which cut through the mountainous centre of the country straight to Herat. This was the route we took.

This was the caravan route. The route of donkeys and camels. This direct route proved to be as difficult as predicted. We had to climb peak after peak meeting occasional camel caravans or shepherds with their flocks of sheep when we were near a village. After climbing a peak, we would sit down on some rocks completely out of breath and gain strength to climb the next. We each carried an old army water bottle, but sometimes water was scarce. We saw mirages in the dry desert between the peaks. Blisters became my constant companions and every evening Prabhakar would perform a minor operation on my feet with scissors, plaster and hot water. One day in the mountains my feet became so swollen that the pain was unbearable. I walked ten steps then had to sit down. We were being guided by a local horseman and he insisted that I should sit on his horse, I said, "From Delhi till now I have walked every inch and I don't want to give up." He laughed, saying that I shouldn't be so dogmatic since the body was the most important thing to carry out the walk.

Our average speed on mountain paths was two and a half miles per hour. One day we left at 5 a.m. We met peak after peak, and not a single village. When we started to climb a peak we hoped and expected to see a village from the top but when we arrived at the top of the peak we saw another peak and no sign of any habitation. So it went on, peak after peak, and hour after hour. We must have crossed at least fifteen peaks. By three or four in the afternoon we finished all our water.

93

Sometimes we did see a village in the valley but when we arrived there we discovered only ruins. By sunset we were really worried. Now we had to continue walking in the dark − and if we were to get lost in these mountains who would ever find us? We had seen nobody all day, but we kept on walking. We were hungry, thirsty and exhausted. At about nine in the evening we heard a few dogs barking. Our faces lit up, "There must be a village." We followed the sound of barking. At the outskirts of the village three or four dogs barked at us loudly. We heard a man calling off the dogs. We approached the voice. He was standing in front of a large black tent. He was a Pathan who had come from the town of Kandhar in the Plains to the south. He was a merchant, travelling by camel, trading in cloths, brass pots, salt and green tea, etc. and fortunately in his journeys to Pakistan he had learnt Urdu, a language very similar to our own. We had very little energy left for talking, but he understood instantly our need for shelter for the night. He made us hot tea, gave us some flat bread with cubes of white sugar, and goat cheese. We slept in his tent.

Next morning the clear yellow sun rays woke us. Our Pathan host was up and ready for his journey. His white turban was tightly bound around his head. He wore a black waistcoat on a loose, big, long shirt and underneath it lavishly pleated baggy trousers gathered in at the ankle above his handmade Afghan shoes with upturned points at the toes and tops of painted leather. We sat together drinking tea, flat bread, cubes of sugar and goat's cheese.

"How is your great leader Gandhi?" the Pathan asked. He was shocked to hear that Gandhi had been assassinated fourteen years ago.

"What a crazy world. The Prophet of Peace was killed by a bullet. The world will never understand the value of such great people. Our beloved leader, Abdul Gaffar Khan, is rotting in a prison of the Pakistani dictators. He is our Gandhi. He is the Lord of Love."

We knew well of the Frontier Gandhi as he is known throughout India. Like Mahatma Gandhi he had struggled for the independence of India with complete adherence to non-violent means − a concept almost unknown among the Pathans, the warriors. Mahatma Gandhi had always said, "Gaffar Khan's achievement is greater than that of any of us. We are teaching non-violence to a people who have no weapons and have a tradition of non-violence behind them. He is Badshah − Lord of the Lords − as he teaches non-violence to a people who carry guns."

Our host said, "I have travelled back and forth so many times that if it were added together it would be more than a journey round the world, but I have done it only for my bread and you are doing it for the peace of the world."

"I am surprised to see that you are an admirer of Gandhi and Gaffar Khan and still carry a gun on your shoulder." I said.

"This gun on my shoulder is like my turban on my head, but I pray to Allah that there will be no need for me to use it as Allah has enabled me to live so far without ever using it."

We came out of the tent and saw the glorious sun making the mud huts of the village shine like gold. The village was in front of us on the slope of a hill. It lay in heavenly peace. No sign of modern civilisation, no cars, no radio, no road, no electricity, no telephone, no machinery whatsoever. Men and women were healthy, handsome and strong. A young woman passed us by going to the river. She carried a huge basket on her back, which hung from a strap round her forehead and reached from her shoulders down past her hips, in it she collected cattle dung and firewood. Her face was fair, gentle and innocent. This woman, I thought, will never go to school, will never travel. She will blossom and wither in this valley, oblivious of political intrigues and nuclear explosions. Our Pathan host is the only connection between this village and the outside world.

We reached Herat, the last town of our Afghan journey. No house was higher than one storey. The whole town appeared to be under one roof, with the dome of the mosque over it. The people were tall, brown and handsome, wearing large white turbans and black embroidered clothes. We walked around and met many Western travellers in search of inner peace and hoping to find it through the fresh smoke of hashish which was openly available. These were the beatniks and the first hippies, singing and playing their guitars, absorbed in the sounds. Many were on their way to India, and when they saw us they surrounded us full of curiosity and questions about the ghats of Benares, sadhus, yogis and meditation. Herat was at the crossroads. We, the Eastern travellers were going to the West to shake off dogmas and sectarianism. They were going to India to break out of intellectual and technological straitjackets, hoping to find wisdom in the simple life of the Ashrams.

The story of two Americans lost in the stormy desert was going around Herat and when the local police commissioner heard about us he approached us and tried to persuade us not to walk but to take a bus. He informed us that at that time there was a particularly bad sand storm raging in the border area of Afghanistan and Iran. We waited a few days in Herat in hope that the storm might subside but when it showed no signs of doing so and we were told that it might take weeks for the storm to pass we decided to leave. Since we insisted on walking, the police commissioner then found a villager who knew the desert tracks to act as our guide. If we hadn't had that friendly villager with us, we would have been unable to find our way out of Afghanistan. There were only 75 miles from Herat to the border but it was the most difficult part of our walk so far. For days we were completely enveloped in the whirling sand storm. We wrapped layers of cloth around our heads, especially covering our nose and mouth, just keeping a little space through which to see and even then the sand found its way to all corners of our bodies.

The sun was defeated by the sand; it was so dark that we had to walk holding the hands of our village guide. With the help of the guide we stayed with various local farmers and village chiefs in their mud houses. We ended the journey staying in a government guest house on the border and next morning crossed into Iran.

We passed through many small villages and usually became the guests of the Dehdar — the village chief, but occasionally there were problems. In Khurmabad we went straight to the Dehdar and found him in his shop. In our broken Persian, we explained to him that we needed some shelter for the night. He asked many questions. Soon a small crowd of villagers gathered round. The Dehdar told us that his house was too small and there was no room for us. We said that we could sleep in the courtyard, but this wasn't acceptable. We waited there for almost half an hour but no-one in the crowd offered to give us shelter. It was the first time we had been refused hospitality. Apparently they suspected us to be spies. Someone in the crowd suggested we should go to the next village. At the next village we found that the Dehdar had gone out somewhere. We asked some villagers where we could find a place to sleep for the night. Again we were refused hospitality. We walked on to seek refuge in the next village where we were more fortunate.

The Caspian Sea on our right, green cotton fields and rows of pomegranate trees on our left and the long track disappearing into the

Demavand mountains through which tunnel after tunnel was being bored as part of a new road to Tehran. One time we had to crawl a few hundred yards through a narrow hole only three feet high and just as we were in the hole we heard shouts of "Danger, danger". We crouched to the side with some workers. A dynamite blast shook the mountain, bringing rocks and dust down around us. Like this we crossed the mountains, and came down into the plains and arrived in the capital of Persia, the city of Tehran.

We went straight to the offices of the Kheyhan International, one of the daily newspapers in English, and told them our story. Next morning there were banner headlines with our pictures and a long article. This made us somewhat of celebritiies. The Indian Embassy and the Indian community in particular received us with enthusiasm.

We had written to the Shah requesting an audience. We were now informed through the Indian Embassy that the Shah would be pleased to receive us. Naturally there were one or two formalities with which we should comply — the customs of the court. The court minister told us that we should present ourselves in black suits with matching ties. Neither of us had worn a suit in our lives and we had no suit of any colour. The Indian ambassador was very eager that we should not miss this opportunity and he offered to provide us with suits. We felt that this was against the spirit of our whole venture, and we should go as we were, in our Indian shirts and tight trousers. We wrote to the minister our sentiments. After an exchange of letters and telephone calls apparently the Shah granted us an exception and we went to see him in our ordinary clothes.

The meeting was cordial. He recalled his own journey to Moscow by plane and warned us that we would have to cross the high, snow covered peaks and passes of the Caucuses and walking would be most difficult since it would be winter when we got there. He avoided talking about the problems of peace, armaments and military pacts and whenever we tried to bring the point he either blamed the big powers or cited the vulnerability of the small nations but he showed great interest in our human endeavour of walking through the world. He wanted to give us money to help in our journey but when we explained that not only did we not accept transport, but also we could not accept money, he laughed and said, "We are the same. I also never carry any money. The shah and the fakir meet on the same ground."

He listened carefully to our route through the rest of Iran and afterwards we discovered that the Shah had informed his people along the way and we were given sumptuous hospitality.

While we were in Tehran we went to the Soviet Embassy to arrange our visas. It seemed much easier for us to have walked through the mountains of Afghanistan and the deserts of Iran than to succeed in obtaining a Soviet visa from these officials. The first time we went, we were told that it would be too cold to walk through Russia between January and April. The second time, the same official repeated his arguments about the cold and the snow and added that our political propaganda against nuclear weapons wasn't necessary in the Soviet Union. The third time he said we would be far more usefully employed if we went to western Europe and America for they were causing the nuclear arms race. The fourth time the official went with us to the Indian Embassy to ask their advice. The First Secretary of the Indian Embassy said that the Indian government wasn't responsible for our beliefs in disarmament and it was up to the Russians whether they gave us a visa or not, but the Indian Embassy in Moscow would give us any help that might be necessary in Russia, as Indian citizens. We returned to the Soviet Embassy. The Russian official then offered us tourist visas for twenty days, provided we went only to big cities and provided that we deposited enough money to cover all our expenses in the USSR with the Intourist agency. We told him we were travelling without money and that we must walk, adding "Till now people have been sympathetic and generous to us everywhere and we have no reason to believe that the Soviet people will be different. The visa is for your satisfaction. If we have no visa we will cross the border without it and if your police arrest us and put us in prison, we will still be in the Soviet Union." The official smiled weakly and told us to return the next day. When we went again we saw the councillor and he told us that he had phoned Moscow, talked to the Soviet Peace Committee and that they had taken responsibility to be our hosts and therefore he was treating our case as an exception, and we were given four-month visas.

Equipped with Soviet visas we happily left Tehran, heading north-west towards the Soviet border. The Indian community had kindly re-equipped us with warm coats, sleeping bags and British-made tough military boots to face the Russian winter.

One cold evening. The sky was clouded. All around us the earth was covered by green dewy grass. Fully wrapped in our warm clothes, we were walking all alone on a deserted road. Nobody seemed to be in a hurry to come out of their homes. All was quiet except the whistling of the wind which was blowing hard. Suddenly a Volkswagen beetle stopped. A man got out. "Would you like a lift?" he asked, to which we replied, "No thank you, we are walking." "Where are you walking to?" "Our final destination is Washington," we replied. "but for tonight the nearest village where we can stay." He looked aghast, he said, "Where have you come from?" "From India." "All the way walking?" "Yes, all the way walking." "Never mind," he said, "it's such a cold evening, getting dark, if you break your vow of walking for one day nobody will know about it, I won't tell anyone and you can stay with me in my home." "It is not a question of anyone knowing but we want to walk." His wife intervened. "The nearest town is Qazwin, fifteen miles away, and before that there is no decent place to stop." The man said to her, "I know, they are followers of Gandhi, who fasted for forty days, these Indians seem to have strong willpower." Turning to us he said, "I give you my address, come and stay with me tomorrow."

When, next afternoon, we arrived at his home, we saw him on his knees on the verandah offering Namaz, head bowed to the ground. We waited at one side but when he looked up and saw us, he leapt up and seemed to completely forget his Namaz. He came to embrace us. "Don't let us disturb you in your prayers," we said. He replied, "Receiving a guest is Namaz in practice. Please come in and let me welcome you as Allah has commanded." He called his friends and family around and we all sat down to the national dish of Persia, Chilo Kebab (Kebabs with rice). We didn't take the kebab but there was for us a sumptuous meal of fruit and nuts and buttered rice.

Next morning he took us to the Hamam, the public bath and arranged a barber to cut our hair and packed our rucksacks with dried fruit and nuts and biscuits. A few hours later on the road he gave us another surprise by appearing with his wife and two daughters with a picnic lunch for us all. We had experienced a hundred days of such wonderful Muslim hospitality in Persia by the time we reached the border.

We saw the frontier guards standing alert equipped with guns and binoculars. The Iranian guards waved a signal, in response to which a Soviet military guard advanced up to the border and opened the gates.

Next moment we were in a different country. It was the 1st January 1963, seven months after we had set out from Delhi. The commander of the Soviet frontier guards made a sweet little speech to receive us, "Your arrival reminds me of Afnasi Nikiten who went to India on foot a few centuries ago. Now you two travellers have come to our country with a message of peace. I hope that soon the boundaries dividing mankind will disappear and we shall be able to realise the ideal of world unity. We will no longer need armies or bombs." A message from the central office of the Peace Council in Moscow was waiting for us saying that it would be extremely difficult for us to travel on foot during the winter months and that we shouldn't worry about our expenses since the Council was willing to bear all responsibility for our transport. We were advised to come to Moscow directly by plane. Despite the cold, we stuck to our decision to walk.

We walked for forty days through the villages and towns of Armenia, Azarbaizan and Georgia, through the Caucasus mountains and along the Black Sea. By radio and newspaper, people had learnt of our walk – many of them had never seen a foreigner.

One day as we were walking, we passed a tea factory. Some of the workers recognised us from newspaper photographs and asked us to come in to speak to them. A fabulous meal was served. Hundreds of workers gathered around us. We said, "All over the world it is the workers who bear the burden of the bomb. It is they who pay for it in roubles and dollars, francs and pounds. Millions and millions of them, and it is they who will be killed when the bombs are used. Therefore it is the workers who should raise their voice against the bomb. Workers of the world unite to stop the arms race. You have nothing to lose but bombs." Then a woman ran to the store and brought four packets of tea. She said to us, "What you are saying, I fully agree with – every word. Here are four packets of tea made in our factory. Please give one each to Kruschev, de Gaulle, Macmillan and Kennedy. Tell them that if they get mad in their minds and think of pushing the button to drop nuclear bombs, they should stop for a moment and have a fresh cup of tea from these packets. That will give them a chance to remember that the simple workers of the world want bread and not bombs, want life and not death." Everyone applauded her words.

A few days later we came to Idzewan, the town where the first socialist soviet was declared during the revolution. As we approached it, hundreds of people came to greet us, bringing food, sweets, chocolate and Lenin badges and took us to the centre of the town, where we spoke to several thousand people. Later we stayed with the head of a collective farm. On our arrival his youngest daughter brought towel, soap and a bowl of hot water to wash our feet. I was embarrassed. She insisted, "It is our custom to make a guest feel at home." She took off my shoes and socks and with her soft hands and warm water bathed my aching feet with ceremonial delicacy. Then her father took us out into the garden. He wanted us to inaugurate the wine season and to be the guests of honour. Menon and I dug up a large barrel of wine buried under the ground, and then filled the glasses of the thirty people who had been invited for dinner. I was asked to propose a toast for peace and to empty the glass in one gulp. It was a difficult moment. I said, "No, I don't drink." Someone said, "Here wine is the only drink — water is for washing." Everyone was quiet, holding their glasses ready, looking at us expectantly. After a few moments of panic and confusion, I seized the glass and emptied it down my throat. There was a roar of applause. Dinner that night lasted for six hours. Toast after toast was proposed. One of the daughters asked me to dance. I had never danced before, but she took my hand. The whole atmosphere grew madder and madder. I sang songs of Tagore. One of the young women who was in the party came next morning and said, "I could not sleep all night and kept thinking of your walk and Peace. Can I join in your journey? I will come with you all the way to Washington." We were stunned. This young Armenian girl in her early twenties was firmly convinced that it was right for her to leave everything behind and come with us. Friends and neighbours listening became alarmed and told us that it would be impossible for her to get a passport. We suggested that she should come with us for a few days before committing herself. She had come prepared with her ruck-sack.

She walked with us that day. When we stopped in the next town, her mother came to us and begged us not to take her daughter with us, as she was her only daughter and her only support. The members of the local peace committee and party officials also discouraged both her and us. So the next day she was not there.

In our Georgian journey we arrived at Gori, the birth place of Stalin. At that time Krushchev had much discredited Stalin, but the people of Gori were proud of him. A giant statue stood in the market square, although in other towns they had been dismantled. The museum devoted to him was still open to visitors and our host, a member of the local Peace Group, told us that he had some difficulty in convincing people there about the atrocities perpetrated by Stalin.

We were put up in a small guest house. We were deeply asleep when we heard someone knocking. Prabhakar went to the door. "I am a taxi-driver. I saw you walking with your banners. I read your leaflet. You are good boys." He got 20 roubles out of his pocket. "This is my day's earning. I want to give it to you to support your cause". The conversation seemed interesting so I joined Prabhakar. "Thank you, but we are sorry, we do not carry money, we cannot accept money. Please don't feel that we are rejecting your help and support", we said in our primitive Russian. "Why not?", he protested. "I too am against our bombs. It's no good Kruschev talking about peace and blaming the West for the arms race. If there has to be war, let us fight a conventional war. At least in it we can show some courage, some ingenuity, but there is no war skill in dropping nuclear bombs on sleeping people, so let me give you these roubles as the contribution of an insignificant taxi driver".

"We are delighted to hear your words and your words are worth more than hundreds of roubles. Please don't insist on giving us money. We have taken a vow not to handle it on our journey."

"Alright then, please don't walk tomorrow, I will take you to wherever you are going in my taxi."

"Oh dear," I said to Prabhakar, "how can we make him understand that that is also against our vow?". The man was disappointed to know that he could be of no practical help to us. He left, wishing us luck.

By the time we reached Sochi on 12 February, the Soviet Peace Committee in Moscow seemed worried. They flew a special messenger who tried to convince us that it was impossible to cross the high ranges of the Ural mountains in mid-February because all the roads were blocked with snow. He argued that we should fly direct to Moscow. We said, "If the roads are blocked, we will stay somewhere in a village until they are cleared". But Mr Paladin replied, "You know nothing of the Russian winter, and you'll be stuck here for months." "So be it," I said, "we are not in a hurry. It is already mid-February, let us spend two months by the Black Sea meeting and talking to people and then we can head towards Moscow." This idea did not please him at all. There was something uncomfortable about our peace propaganda to this Peace Committee official. After four days of argument we found ourselves in a stalemate. He explained, "The roads are blocked with snow. The Peace Committee cannot take responsibility for you in such climatic conditions, nor can the Soviet Government allow you to proceed on foot. You are in our country and you must accept our advice." His 'advice' came as an order.

We were to fly over the mountains and land on the other side at Voronesh. But as we were crossing the mountains in the plane, an announcement was made which the peace representative interpreted in English as: "Due to bad weather conditions, the plane cannot land at Voronesh and has to fly straight to Moscow". None of the other passengers seemed at all affected. We suspected that the Peace Committee representative had deliberately misled us and we landed in Moscow in despair. A car awaited us. We were driven to the centre of the city and put up at Hotel Budapest.

Not knowing what to do we telephoned the First Secretary of the Indian Embassy and walked immediately to his house, although it was ten o'clock at night. We told him how our walk had been frustrated and asked him if he would help us to go to Voronesh by train, so that we could walk back to Moscow. "It is Russia, nothing you can do". He made a helpless gesture with his hands.

Although deeply upset, we had to live with the fait accompli. The Peace Committee went out of their way to organise visits to the Bolshoi, museums and a journey to Yasnaya Polyana, the birthplace of Leo Tolstoy. No effort was spared in their attempts to reconcile us to our forcible abduction from Sochi. They organised meetings, interviews with newspapers and radio, dialogue with politicians and even a message of greeting from Kruschev himself. But it soon became clear that in spite of the Peace Committee's lavish hospitality in Moscow, that they never accepted our plan to walk freely through the villages of Russia. The visas we had obtained from the Soviet Embassy at Teheran were valid till April 1963, but one day the authorities took our passports from our hotel without informing us, cancelled the previous visas and instead gave us visas due to expire on 14 March.

The officials of the Peace Committee tried to persuade us that we had spent long enough in their country. They said they were arranging for us a free flight from Moscow to Warsaw so that we could make more profitable use of our time elsewhere. Next day a Peace Committee interpreter arrived with two plane tickets. We refused to accept them and made it quite clear that we had no desire to resort to any transport for our journey — except our legs. Any more discussion with the Peace Committee was pointless. We went directly to the visa officials. They told us they had received a letter from the Peace Committee that we were going to Warsaw by plane and accordingly they had made the necessary changes in our visas. If we wanted to have our visas in their original form, we would have to get a letter from the Peace Committee to that effect and only then could they make alterations. We wrote a letter to the Peace Committee saying that we intended to set out on our march according to our original plan.

13th March 1963. It was evening and darkness had fallen. We put our rucksacks on our backs and came out of our hotel. Moscow was covered by a white sheet of snow. With heavy steps we trudged along the streets groping our way in the dim pools of light from the lamp posts. The white masses of snow shimmered in the dark night. We walked out of the city area and found ourselves in the green-belt which was pitch black and uninhabited. We went to the trolley-bus terminus to try and sleep there, but at midnight a woman came to lock it up and asked us to leave. We suggested that she lock it from outside and leave us inside for the night, then in the morning we would go on. She couldn't understand why we didn't have anywhere to sleep. She remembered reading about us in *Pravda*, so she took us to the Hotel Ukraina, a huge skyscraper hotel, where she knew somebody. She explained the situation to him and he gave us a room for the night.

Next morning we set out on our journey ignoring the fact that our visas expired that day. Every time we saw a police car or a police man we feared arrest. But mysteriously nothing happened. We felt liberated to come out of the maze of Moscow's skyscrapers, to roam once again through the Russian countryside, to be among the warm and hospitable villagers and farmers. The country surrounding Moscow had witnessed many a bloody battle. The wounds of the last war were still fresh and would start bleeding at the slightest pressure. "Both my father and brother fell in the war. Now I am completely alone," someone said. "I lost one of my legs in the war. It crippled me for life," another said. "I lost my eyes, my one hand in the war — and though I go on living, my life is of no use to anyone." We often heard such sad remarks. Once we were staying in a house where only two women lived. All the male members of the family had been killed in the war. In another village an old couple had lost all their sons and were now living alone with their memories from the past.

Another time in a small village we met a farmer, his eyes rested on us for some time before he decided to speak. "They say you are the messengers of peace. You are coming from India and will go to America. Is it true? Will you convey my message to the American people? Will you tell them that though they fought in the war, the actual war was never fought in their country. The very thought of war seems nightmarish to us . . . " He spoke for a long time with great passion. After he finished, he took us in his arms and kissed us.

The temperature was 30 degrees centigrade below freezing point but we were convinced that if the common Russian people could perform their daily work in winter, we could at least manage to stay alive. Sometimes the freezing wind blowing from Siberia made our bodies numb and every step forward a torture. We had never experienced such biting cold in our lives, nor had we ever seen such masses of snow which enveloped the entire world around us. We would walk for ten miles until our bodies felt like stone, as if our blood had stopped moving then we would desperately look for some place to warm ourselves. I had icicles from my nose, my moustache and beard were frozen solid. Although we had been given fur coats and caps by the kind Russian people, no clothes could be made to keep out the Russian cold.

Once a peasant invited us to spend the night at his house. His wife had gone out on some errand, so our host cooked food and made up beds for us. When his wife returned, our host whispered to her in the kitchen that we were going to stay with them for the night. She didn't approve and refused to have anything to do with us. There was a long heated argument between husband and wife and the wife burst into tears. "This is a home not a guest house. You keep bringing strange people here. I can't bear it. If you want them to stay then I will go."

The husband stalked out of the kitchen, saying over his shoulder, "Do what you like, I won't stop you."

Before we could intervene, the wife took their baby in her arms and rushed out into the cold. We, 'the messengers of peace', had caused trouble in a family. We got ready to find shelter elsewhere.

"Where can you go at this hour?" the peasant said in despair. "It's pitch dark outside and the streets are full of mud and sleet."

He thought a while, then went out. A little later he reappeared and told us a friend of his had agreed to put us up. Holding each other's hands, we stumbled through the mud along the dark lanes. The man kept apologising to us and cursing his wife. We said, "Don't worry, we have had such marvellous hospitality from Russian people, that a little walk now to find a bed is no trouble to us." At his friend's house everyone had gone to sleep, but the farmer there woke up his two children and made them sleep on one bed. Prabhakar and I took the other one. Next morning they made a large warm breakfast for us. The wife said, "Why don't you stay here longer? After walking for so long, won't it be better to take some rest?" But we went on.

Forty-five days from Moscow, after four months in the Soviet Union, we reached the border. The Custom Officer examined our passports. "You have been in this country illegally. Your visas expired long ago", he said to us. "Where have you been all this time?" We told him the whole story, but he wasn't satisfied and telephoned someone in Moscow. We thought that now the time had come to face the consequences of ignoring the authorities and anticipated being arrested. All along, our way of travelling puzzled the Russians. They didn't know quite how to deal with us. The customs official turned and shrugged his shoulders. "You've done some strange things, but you're going anyway. It's too late, no point in keeping you here any longer. Daswidaniya! (Goodbye)."

On the 1st May we arrived in Poland. Through Warsaw, Posnan and many other towns we enjoyed the friendship and generosity of the Polish people The winter was left behind and it was now sunny summer. Once, to rest from the heat of the midday, we went into a school and found a few teachers to chat to during their lunch break. This was not acceptable to the disciplinarian headmaster who came and said, "the school is not a chatting house", and asked us to leave. Shocked and embarrassed, we stumbled out and found some shade under a tree. A child, watching the incident, seeing the headmaster disappear, came and asked us from where we came. "India". He looked in one of his books and found a picture of the Taj Mahal — "Is this where you come from, the country of the Taj Mahal?" "Yes", we said.

"Oh, what a shame, I always wanted to go to India, but now I can't". "Why not?" we asked. "When you come to my country, my village, my school, you are treated so badly, how can I possibly dare to come to your country?" . We said, "It is not your fault. You can still come". "Not unless I see that you receive hospitality here. Can you come to my home for tea?" "Where is your home?" "This way", he pointed eastward back along the road we had travelled. "We must head westwards. Your home is not in our direction". "If you can walk from India to Poland, a couple of miles extra is nothing to you." He was almost in tears. He could not have been older than twelve or thirteen, but he was so persistent that we followed him. "Mummy, mummy, look who I have brought − the people from India, the country of the Taj Mahal, where I will go one day". His mother was as much pleased.

With such rich experiences we passed through Poland and arrived in East Germany.

A thorough check of documents and rucksacks was made when we arrived at the East Berlin city border. The faces of the Russian and German soldiers were tense. They seemed to be performing their duties so mechanically and without heart that we started talking to them. In the beginning they were sceptical of our peace talk, but suddenly one of them burst out − "You're right. We have no peace of mind here at home or at the front. We are longing for the day when we can throw away all these arms and join you in the fight for peace." He was an East German soldier in uniform guarding the border of a tensely divided city at a crisis point in the cold war − it was just before President Kennedy was due to visit West Berlin. The other four soldiers looked at him as though he were mad to talk in such a way to strangers.

Through West Berlin and East Germany, we arrived in West Germany. One evening we were looking for shelter. We saw a very impressive church and beside it the minister's house. We knocked at the door of the house. In the door there was a little spy hole and we could hear that someone was looking through it. A moment later the minister opened the door a few inches and we could see the edge of his gown, the bible in his hand and his frowning face. We offered our leaflet which was in German and which explained who we were and what we were doing. He didn't accept it. "What do you want?" he nervously asked. "Some shelter for the night". "No place here, go away", he banged the door. We thought there must be some mistake and we

107

knocked again hoping to explain ourselves properly. He opened the door and shouted firmly, "Don't knock at my door. There is no place here, go away immediately." He gave us no chance to explain anything. We felt sorry at distressing him and left.

A few hundred yards away we found the police station. Not knowing what to do we went in. A young policeman smiled at us. "What can I do for you?" "May we sit down for a few moments, we will explain to you?" He shook hands and offered us comfortable chairs. We gave him our leaflet, which he read carefully and asked in a curious voice, "Is this really true? How long did it take you to walk from India to here?" We quickly came to the point that our most urgent need at the moment was to find shelter for the night and could he suggest anywhere. He thought for a moment, then lifted the telephone and rang somewhere. Receiving an affirmative answer, he said, "All right, come with me". We went back past the church and arrived at a house. It was a hospital. "You don't mind sleeping in a hospital for the night, do you?" and he handed us over to the nurse in charge. We were taken aback — this was the first time we had stayed in a hospital. The nurses were very kind. We had a sumptuous meal of fruit, vegetables, milk cheese and bread. Next morning not only were we given a large breakfast, but also some sandwiches to take away with us. We passed once again the church and the police station and waved goodbye to the good-hearted policeman.

After walking through Hannover, Dusseldorf and Cologne, we arrived in Bonn. We had written a letter to Chancellor Adenauer, asking for an appointment. We had talked about German problems with the Minister of Foreign Affairs in East Germany and we wanted to have similar talks with West German officials. When we arrived in Bonn, we went to the Chancellor's office. After we had waited there for a long time, we were asked to come next day. When we went there next day, we were again asked to come the next day. Finally, on the third day, we were told that neither the Chancellor nor any other official would be able to meet us 'due to political reasons'.   Since no government official was willing to see us, we decided to stage a demonstration in front of the Chancellor's office. We arrived there at nine in the morning. Just after our arrival the police also appeared and snatched everything away — placards, books and leaflets — and we had no alternative but to squat there empty-handed. This was typical of the treatment we received in West Germany. All along government officials were suspicious of our activities. We were stopped from distributing leaflets by the police on more than one occasion, and were questioned frequently by plainclothes security officers. Even our hosts were harrassed by them.

From Germany we walked through Belgium, then northern France and arrived in Paris on 5 August.

While we were walking through Belgium, Russia, America and Great Britain signed a nuclear test ban treaty. President de Gaulle refused to sign it, saying that until there was complete disarmament France would go ahead with her atomic tests. We sent a letter to President de Gaulle, but received no answer. We wrote two more letters with no better result, so we announced our decision to demonstrate in a non-violent and peaceful manner in front of the Elysee Palace. News of our plan had spread through France and even beyond, and two young men from Germany and Denmark, Wolfgang and Ole, came to join us.

Our friends had advised us not to go on foot to the President's house since the police might arrest us on the way, so the four of us went by car. Many journalists and photographers had gathered and the police were everywhere. We got out of the car just in front of the palace and started to open our banner. 'BAN THE BOMBS AND STOP THE TESTS'. But as we were unfolding it, the banner was snatched from our hands by the police who had surrounded us. The chief of the palace security came down the steps and invited us inside. The atmosphere was tense, the police pushed us into the palace and barred the way to the press. We were taken to a palatial room.

"You are creating a disturbance in Paris," the security chief said.

We asked him "Please inform the President of our demand to see him."

"The President has received your letters and even knows where you are at present, but is unable to meet you."

We said, "The only choice left to us is to go on demonstrating."

He replied, "You cannot change the government's policy."

"Nor can the government change ours," we said.

A few minutes later we were pushed into a heavily guarded police van and driven out of the palace through the back gate to a police station. We were put in an underground, semi-circular cell. After two hours of interrogation the police officer said, "I'll let you go if you promise not to go to the President's house again."

"Unless we get an assurance from the government that France will not conduct nuclear tests, we cannot leave Paris or the Elysee Palace."

Next we were taken to the police headquarters where we had to wait for another two hours. It was 9.30 pm when we were taken to a police lock-up. We didn't know what was going to happen. Late that night we were put in cells. The cells were dirty, freezing cold and the air heavy with strange smells. There were two damp mattresses on the floor, stained and sticky, and no blankets or sheets. All our possessions had been taken away and we were left with the barest minimum of clothes, minus the cords which held up our loose Indian trousers. The only other thing in the cell, right beside the mattresses, was an open toilet which stank.

It was the first time I had been in such a place. Everything we had worked and walked against was institutionalised in one place — fear and mistrust alive everywhere, in the walls, the locks, the sounds. The deterioration of the human situation was terrible — an old man shaking and stuttering on the stairs, a drunkard shouting and the police kicking and beating him, ill and disturbed people screaming out all night. I had thought of Paris as one of the most civilised and rich cities in the world and seeing humanity on the most degraded level — it was a shock — like being thrown from the top of a mountain. We had been roaming freely like the wind and suddenly we were blocked and locked into an eight-foot square cell. All night there was the glare of a light-bulb. We were unable to sleep, minds spinning round and round. Was this the final point of our journey? How long would we be here? From Delhi to Paris was one long road ending in prison. All the colours, green forests, brown mountains, white snow, yellow fruit and blue lakes and seas — flashed through my mind in the dark gloomy stinking atmosphere of the lock-up.

Next morning while in the washroom, we managed to have a few words with Wolfgang and Ole and decided to make a hunger strike as a protest against the treatment and conditions of the place. For two days we refused to eat the food that was pushed into our cell — porridge, bread, meat and potatoes. I could fast, wait and meditate, I had learnt it during my monkhood. On the second day we felt the bite of hunger — the tongue, the teeth and the throat were dry and sour. Prabhakar was very weak and lay on a mattress unable to do anything. I massaged his back, chest and head helping him to relax and feel the body. I had always felt closeness with him, but in this closed prison cell I felt even closer − a sense of unity and togetherness that had gradually evolved during the walk.

On the third day we were taken to the police officer. Two officials of the Indian Embassy were there.

The police officer said, "You're a problem for us. Inside you'll die and outside you'll sit in front of the palace, and we are inundated with the phone calls of your supporters."

He handed us our passports, a deportation order and two air tickets, saying, "Tomorrow morning you leave Paris by Air France for Delhi."

We had walked from Delhi to Paris in sixteen months and we were going to be flown back in sixteen hours and that was the end of it. We tried to change the police officer's decision to send us to Delhi, but it was no use. So we spoke in Hindi to the embassy officials, asking them to do something. They talked to the police officer, saying that it would create 'a serious misunderstanding' between France and India and bad publicity for France. They asked that we be handed over to them and guaranteed that they would get us out of France within twenty-four hours. The police officer agreed. The choice for us was either to be deported to India by plane or leave France by train for England. In the circumstances we decided to compromise.

As we came out of the room we saw Madame Petit, one of those who had demonstrated with us. She had been arrested on 16 September for distributing our leaflets but was later released. When she saw how weak and worn out we looked, she asked permission to bring us some fruit, biscuits, potato-chips and coffee for us. Then we were taken back to our cell.

Next day we were taken to the police officer again. The Indian ambassador himself was there to make arrangements for our 'deportation' to England. Afterwards he drove us to his home, gave us a sumptuous supper and saw us onto the train to Dover, handing over two tickets. Wolfgang and Ole were deported to their respective countries by plane.

Ever since we had been in western Europe, people involved in anti-war movements had provided hospitality and organised publicity in many places. The nature of our walk had changed — the almost daily adventures in the East of finding food and shelter and the unexpected encounters of hospitality were replaced by the less eventful demands for publicity and lectures. London was the mecca of the peace movement and we received wholehearted support and co-operation from many peace organisations and activists. CND, Committee of One Hundred, War Resisters International, the Quakers — all identified with our walk. *Peace News* had been covering it since the beginning and people were waiting for us to arrive. We were surrounded by friends, supporters and admirers, and to find hospitality was no longer a problem. National newspapers wrote feature articles, radio and television interviewed us. Also we were driven to see Bertrand Russell in his Welsh home.

In London we were once again entangled in the complicated web of visas and passports for America. At last after twenty-two days of waiting, we got through the formalities and were given visas. Although we had decided to go to Washington, we could never sort out how to cross the Atlantic. We always said, "When it comes, we shall see." *Peace News* started an Atlantic fund for us and all the money we received from television, radio and lectures was put in it; advertisements in peace magazines brought further contributions to the boat voyage. There was more than enough money for two transatlantic tickets. We walked to Southampton and on the morning of 22 November boarded the Queen Mary bound for New York. Here we were, two travellers without any money, on one of the most luxurious liners in the world, with a separate cabin to ourselves, and a bell to call a waiter at any time to bring specially cooked vegetarian meals.

Going into the unknown world and confronting it without a penny in my pocket meant that all the differences between rich and poor, educated and illiterate vanished and a real life beneath all these divisions emerged. Whether I slept in a comfortable bed or on the floor of a barn or under a tree, it didn't make any difference. As a wanderer I was free of shadows from the past and I knew nothing of the status of the people I met. The experience of beautiful emptiness within myself, with neither material nor spiritual possessions, unlocked my soul. I had no ambitions to fulfill as a result of the walk. It was a journey without destination; journey and destination became one, thought and action became one. I felt myself moving like a river. A river and its flow are not separate things, I and my movement were not separate. The journey was me. It was as much an inner journey as an outward one. It was a journey into detachment. The contradiction between movement and stillness ceased. I was on the move in stillness, a journey in stillness.

I was a wanderer, wandering through life, living from day to day, from inspiration to inspiration, from emotion to emotion. I become involved with people and situations, but my commitment was never to that particular person or situation but to the flow in which the experience took place. In wandering, in spite of all crises, I survived and was sustained.

In wandering I felt a sense of union with the whole sky, the infinite earth and sea. I felt myself as part of the cosmic existence. It was as if by walking I was making love to the earth itself. Wandering was my path, my true self, my true being. It released my soul-force, it brought me in relation to everything else. I stood like I stand in front of the mirror. People, nature, everything became like a mirror and I could see myself in them, what I was. I was born in a dream of wandering, a seed conceived in my mother. My dreams are of wandering. From birth I was wandering − as a monk, with Vinoba, and in the walk − whatever I learnt came through wandering.

My two legs were the most creative parts of my body and the most creative expression of my energy. Without these two legs I would have been a zero. But with my two legs there was no place in the world that I could not go. There is a story of God freeing the world with his legs. An evil king was dominating the world. God who wanted to destroy him came in the form of a dwarf and asked the king if he would give a little thing. The king said, "What do you want?" The dwarf replied, "Let me walk three steps and whatever space of land I cover give me that land." The king laughed, "I have the whole earth under my rule, so walk three steps and take the land." The dwarf put one step in heaven and the other on the serpent's head which holds up the earth and thus encompassed the two ends of the universe, then said, "Where can I have my third step?" And he put his foot on the head of the demon king.

Throughout the walk people everywhere were busy in their own day-to-day existence. We went knocking on their doors. The spirit was there but it had gone to sleep. Over and over again at the most intimate point of the conversation, people would say with a voice of deep despair and sometimes almost crying, "You are right but we can do nothing." But when we two came from distant lands with a little love and peace that gave them a shudder and made them forget their day-to-day problems for a while and listen and share.

As far as politicians were concerned, in every capital we tried to meet the head of state by writing letters, telephoning and even going personally to their offices. But apart from the Shah of Persia we only met less important government officials. In a conversation with the Chairman of the Supreme Soviet, Spiridonov, in Moscow, we were confronted with a rigid attitude that was obviously the reason why prime ministers and heads of state thought it a waste of time talking to us personally. Spiridonov said, "We cannot take any risk of unilateral disarmament. Suppose we disarm unilaterally and the opposite party threatens to destroy our system, what will happen? Unless the other party is prepared to disarm, we can do nothing. I agree that militarism is the very opposite to the real concept of communism or of democracy for that matter, but today we are helpless. Out of necessity and fear, we have to build and maintain a large machinery to defend the nation and to preserve peace in the world." In all the countries politicians, soldiers and people in responsible jobs argued: "We're all right, we're peaceful. The other party is the trouble-maker." The Russians said, "Go to the West"; Westerners said, "Go to the communists"; Pakistanis said, "Go and clean your own country." Always the other, the other . . .

We met no-one on the walk who didn't want peace, but no-one has the power to decide about peace and war. When it comes down to it, politicians are as powerless as the common people. No political or army commander said that he wanted war, but everybody had to maintain the machinery of war. In other words, there is no alternative. As long as people go on acting from the premise of fear, there can be no alternative. The politician says that by maintaining an army and nuclear weapons, he is preserving the freedom of his country. But that freedom is illusory since the expenditure of the gross national income of one country entirely depends on the other country's expenditure. Instead of acting independently, a country has always to react, depending on

114

another country's activities, which creates a dangerous sense of powerlessness in politicians as much as in the common people.

We couldn't convince people to accept our arguments. Argument merely breeds argument and everyone has their own answer. But walking as we were, going from country to country, to different cultures and religions, going in jungles, forests and mountains without weapons, even against the animals, we were perhaps able to communicate a sense of the inner power of the individual and the loss of fear of 'the other'.

Many times during our walk people had pressed us to accept money. At Jalalabad in Afghanistan the editor of a daily paper told us that he would like to help us in the name of peace and tried to give some Afghan money. At Kabul we were talking with a shopkeeper who was so impressed that he took a handful of bank notes out of his cash box and put them in front of us. When we refused to take the money, he presented us with two writing pens. In Sukhumi, a Georgian town, the representative of the Soviet Peace Committee was shocked to find that we were without money. "Take these forty roubles," he tried to persuade us, "You can use it in times of emergency."

Because we weren't carrying any money, people were more concerned to look after our basic needs. When we reached Kabul two friends from India sent us some warm clothes to carry us through the cold weather of Afghanistan, and our host in Kabul presented each of us with a fur cap and a pair of warm shoes. In Behsaher someone saw us walking in worn-out, tattered shoes. He asked us to wait and after some time he came back with two pairs of brand new shoes. In Tehran an Indian merchant bought us sleeping-bags, pullovers, winter shoes and coats, saying, "Take whatever you need. I am only the trustee of the wealth I possess."

For two and a half months, between Kabul and Tehran, we were completely cut off from friends in India and from any news of what was happening in the world. Occasionally our hosts in different countries helped us to post letters; at other times we would carry letters with us and whenever any car stopped to ask if we wanted a lift, we would ask them to stamp our letters and post them instead. This happened a lot in Russia, especially with lorry drivers. At Tabriz the postmaster-general presented us with a large pile of airletters. And when we stayed in some house, our host invariably gave us a cake of soap, razor-blades, stamps and other things we needed for our daily use. In one village in Russia our host didn't have any safety-blades but only a cut-throat razor, so he himself shaved off our beards.

When you have nothing you can give everything, including yourself, without withholding anything and you can receive everything without doubting the generosity of the giver.

The Queen Mary brought us to the port of New York where we were met by the anti-war activists of America. Two of them were to walk with us on the last trek, New York – Washington. John Papworth flew from London to walk with us. The five of us started from New York on 7 December 1963.

Long back when we were passing through the Khyber Pass, four American tourists stopped their car and offered us a lift.

"No thanks, we're walking," we said.

"Where are you going?" they asked.

"To America."

They burst into laughter. "D'you know where America is?"

"We've only seen it on the map," we replied.

One of them gave us his address and telephone number saying jokingly, "If you ever reach America call me."

Walking through Philadelphia in two feet of snow, we telephoned him. "D'you remember two Indians you met in the Khyber Pass?"

"Where are they?"

"We're here, in your town."

He couldn't believe it.

"We hope to see you tomorrow morning," we said, since it was almost midnight.

"I can't wait till tomorrow, I'm coming now." His first words when he saw us were, "So your dream came true."

In Washington we had wanted to make an appeal to ·President Kennedy. However, when we eventually reached there on 9 January 1964, after walking 8,000 miles, President Kennedy had been killed, the victim of an assassin's bullet. It was to the cemetery and not to the White House that we went to look for him. And it was at his tomb, where the young president had ended his journey that our walk also came to an end – a long walk from Gandhi's grave to Kennedy's grave. Never during the walk did I feel such a sense of desolation and weariness as when I faced the tomb of the dead Kennedy. As we stood in silence, soft drops of rain fell on the flame burning there. The hair on my body stood on end as I shivered. It had been raining when we had started from Gandhi's grave. We had walked from the other side of the world for peace, and had come to America, a symbol of military power. At Kennedy's grave there was neither peace nor war, but something beyond — a moment of complete stillness. Gandhi and Kennedy. Kennedy and Gandhi. The grave, the bullet, the rain. The rain and the flame became one. The moment of beginning and ending became one.

The walk was finished. It did not bring peace to the world, it brought peace to me. We had one wish to fulfil, to see the great man of action and thought — Martin Luther King. We said goodbye to our two American friends who had walked with us from New York; they were so happy with walking for peace that they continued walking across America. John Papworth, Prabharkar and myself went south to Atlanta.

A short round faced man was sitting behind a simple office desk. He was talking on the telephone, and we waited. When he was finished he said, "I have to spend half of my life on the telephone", and he laughed. It was Martin Luther King. Our conversation grew. He said, "My non-violence is a revolutionary non-violence, my non-violence touches the deepest corner of human consciousness. I am convinced that we will win. We will bring an end to all discrimination and division." His words flowed from his mouth like a fountain. Silently listening to him I felt renewed and refreshed — all that walk was worthwhile just to come and see him.

From Atlanta we went to Albany to meet some of the workers of the Civil Rights movement. There John and I went to a cafe. It was elegantly decorated and comfortable. We found a quiet corner and sat down. A waitress in a white apron came to take our order. "Tea and cheese sandwiches for two, please", John announced. The waitress went. We became immersed in our conversation. The waitress came again and said, "Sorry we have no tea and cheese sandwiches". "Can we have coffe then?", John inquired. "No, we have nothing, sir". The waitress disappeared quickly. We went to the manager who was standing at the cash counter. "Can't we have a cup of tea?", we asked. He said, "No, you can't. Please leave immediately." We said, "Isn't this a cafe to serve the public?" "It's my cafe and I serve whom I like," he replied. "We don't leave here without a cup of tea", I said. His face became red and his lips swollen, and his breath became short, fast and loud. He pulled open a drawer and took out a pistol. Pointing it at me, he said. "Are you getting out, or should I teach you a lesson?" "There is no need for your gun, nor for your anger. I just want a cup of tea", I said anxiously. John stepped in between us and covered my body with his. The waiters and waitresses and various customers gathered round and pushed John and I away, out of the cafe. I felt sorry that I caused anger and upset the manager, but John was furious and wrote a letter of protest to the Secretary of State. Eventually I was informed that the office of the Secretary of State had apologised to the Indian Ambassador for the incident.

I did not regret the affair. It had enabled me to experience the depths of tension which had given birth to the Klu Klux Klan on the one hand and to the Black armed revolutionaries on the other. How difficult was the task of a sane social reformer like Martin Luther King. He had always to walk on a tight rope between the two.

We received a letter from the War Resisters of Japan, asking us, "How can you complete your journey without visiting the only victim of the Bomb against which you've been walking?" They were right and we agreed to return to India via Japan. Air tickets were bought with the money raised from our lectures.

We arrived in the country of the Rising Sun to find Buddhist monks, Christian pacifists and students at the airport to greet us. We were taken to a trade union hall near the airport to tell our story. A married couple and two young female students who were at the meeting spontaneously offered to walk with us and act as our interpreters and guides. An American pacifist woman, Mary Harvey, flew from America to join us in our pilgrimage to Hiroshima.

Under the glare of television cameras and press photographers, we left the centre of Tokyo. Tokyo seemed to be an unending city, we passed into Yokohama without noticing. We stayed in a guest house there, where we were received by the Mayor. After ceremonial speeches he presented us discreetly with an envelope tied with a red ribbon which contained a few thousand yen – a support for peace. Nearly everyone who came to meet us brought some present – calligraphy, wall hangings, door hangings, drawings and paintings, and dolls. We were overloaded but fortunately someone took responsibility to send these gifts on to India.

We had our first experience of a Japanese public bath, which later became an essential part of our daily routine. I had never seen so many naked bodies together and I was shy to take off my pants – in India we would never be naked in public, and we would always wear pants when taking a shower. First we would wash our bodies sitting on a little low wooden stool by a warm tap, soaping ourselves and rinsing with bowls of water. Then we soaked our bodies in a small swimming pool filled with near boiling water. There was a thin bamboo wall which separated the men's from the women's areas and one woman sitting in the doorway was in charge of both. When we had completed our bath, we put on cotton kimonos provided by the guest house. On a summer evening the majority of people would be walking around after their baths in these comfortable kimonos.

The Japanese dinner was always a delight. Bowl after bowl after bowl of soup, rice, vegetables and pickles with a touch of seaweed, soya sauce and tofu. My Japanese friends would break into laughter seeing me failing to use their beautifully decorated chopsticks. The dish I enjoyed most was tempura, a variety of vegetables enveloped in batter and fried, but of course when sukiyaki was arranged I was happiest. Then I could choose exactly what I wanted to eat and hear no grumbles about my vegetarianism and the Japanese love of fish and fish-eggs. Freshly chopped vegetables of every kind were provided and I could cook them myself. The only thing I missed was some good brown bread and milk. But everything   was forgotten when I was given tea to drink. Tea before dinner, tea after dinner, tea during dinner, truly every time is tea time. Sometimes it is green tea, other times black tea. If it is summer you drink ice cold barley tea, or in spring time cherry blossom tea. I wish the Coca Cola culture would keep away and leave Japan to tea. 700 miles from Tokyo, we reached the 'peace garden' in Hiroshima on the nineteenth anniversary of the first atomic explosion.

Much of our time during the walk was spent with the peace groups who, although they were very active to bring peace to the world had no peace within themselves. Broadly the peace groups were either Communist or Indepedent. The Communists insisted that America and the capitalist countries were responsible for the peacelessness of the world. They derived their strength from the trade union and therefore they were very powerful. The Independents comprised Anarchists, Christians and Buddhists. Fortunately both groups supported our walk. Always we urged them not to put so much emphasis on their ideological base and instead unite for some common programme. But we were no more successful in bringing peace to them than elsewhere. Only when there is peace within, can the peace without be established. Although the Peace Movement in Japan was stronger than anywhere else, they were no more successful because of their own divideness.

After travelling by boat from Japan to Bombay, once again we stood in front of Gandhi's grave in Delhi. It was the anniversary of Gandhi's birthday (20 October 1964), and people were saying prayers, chanting mantras and turning spinning wheels. There was an autumn sun and a hard wind. As I laid yellow flowers on the black stone of Gandhi's grave, I felt again the presence of his personality — a man of universal love.

From Delhi we went to see Vinoba at his ashram in Pawnar. The ashram is situated on a hill beside a river. We climbed the stone steps. At the top there was a temple and beyond it under the shadow of a large tree Vinoba was sitting on a wooden platform surrounded by members of the ashram. There was the sound of the fast-flowing river and the quiet voice of Vinoba, teaching from the Upanishads. Here was a wise teacher, sharing his knowledge with his disciples in an informal way. When he saw us, Vinoba smiled and beckoned us to sit by him.

Ending his teaching, he put his hand on my shoulder and said, "How are your feet? I heard stories of your blisters." He laughed. "They are the ornaments of walking".

On his face and in his whole presence there was the quietness of dawn. I immediately felt intimacy and warmth.

During our conversation I told him that many people in the West, especially in the peace movement, wanted him to go to Europe and America.

Vinoba looked around and said, "The centre of the universe is here," then with a chuckle added, "The meaning of my name is Ganesh."

I asked what he meant?

Vinoba said, "One day the supreme god Vishnu called all the gods and devils together and said he would give his blessings to the one who went round the earth and was the first to come back. All of them left immediately on their various transports − riding on a lion, a peacock, a swan, a bullock, etc − each one wanting to be the first to return. But the little elephant-faced deity Ganesh, the son of Lord Shiva, was puzzled and thought, "I'll take ages to travel round the earth on my transport of a mouse and I am bound to come last." So he drew a circle on the ground, wrote inside it 'Om Vishnu' and rode around it on his mouse. He returned to Vishnu, who was sitting on his lotus throne, and put his head on Vishnu's feet saying, "I'm the first to return. Give me your blessings." One by one the gods and devils started gathering and awaited eagerly Vishnu's verdict. When everyone had returned, Vishnu gave his blessings to Ganesh. None of the gods could understand how Ganesh on his mouse could have come first and they begged for an explanation. Ganesh said, "What you see in space and time is only an illusion. The real essense of the universe is Vishnu himself. So you don't need to go anywhere to circle the world, the world is here."

We had gone around the world, yet Vinoba was implying that it wasn't necessary to go anywhere.

We went on by train to Bangalore. Lata came to the same place where I had left her almost two and a half years before. As the train drew slowly into the platform, I opened the door of the carriage and stood on the step, my eyes searching for her among the people milling around. Suddenly I saw her dark hair bound in a bunch on the top of her head with a white jasmine flower-ring round it. She was standing with our daughter in her arms and a garland of red roses in one hand. I waved and she came running towards me. We embraced and stood there holding each other. I tried to lift my daughter into my arms to kiss her, but she hid her face in Lata's sari. Lata said, "Darling, this is your papa." She hesitated a moment more before she came to me.

Prabhakar and I stood awkwardly at the taxi rank, our paths about to separate. He got into a three-wheel scooter taxi, and I saw him disappear into the crowds and traffic waving his arms.

Escape

I had travelled round the world, I had talked about peace, I had received publicity in India and abroad, I had been welcomed by the establishment for my 'adventurous journey' and I relished being in the limelight. I returned with great enthusiasm and impatience to act, but the question was — what to do? Going on the walk into an unknown world with a known action proved easier than finding the right action in the known world. During the month in Bangalore with Lata's family I received many letters, particularly from Gramdan workers inviting me to speak about the walk. Lata and I set off with our child on a tour of India. As soon as I stopped walking and started talking I was caught up in the illusion of self importance. After two months Lata became unhappy with the travelling and talking. We went to Benares.

We rented a flat in a beautiful house owned by the Queen of Benares, with a balcony overlooking the Ganges. Here I wrote my first Hindi book "Journey around the world without a Penny" from diaries kept during the walk. The publisher wanted the book as soon as possible, he gave me a typist to whom I dictated the whole book straight onto the typewriter. The pages were sent to the press as soon as they were typed. The book was written in a month and printed in a month. The publisher said never had one of his authors worked so fast nor had he printed so fast. A hardback edition of five thousand copies was sold in six months then the paperback edition of twenty thousand was out. I received more than a thousand letters especially from young people who were inspired and many of whom wanted to undertake a similar trip and asked my advice.

Martin Luther King had given me his book "Stride towards Freedom". Only by translating it into Hindi could I express my deep admiration for him and release the emotion I felt towards him.

Lata started to feel anxious about my writing and my view of life. She said "Whatever you do, the world is not going to change. Wars and exploitation will continue. There have been hundreds of great saints — Buddha and Gandhi — they have come and gone. D'you think that you Satish Kumar, can change the world? You will not change the world, you will only ruin our lives. Stop trying to solve other people's problems and solve your own."

One day we were sitting on the balcony, watching the trains go over the bridge across the Ganges.

She said, "Your revolution is all very well, but now you are married and we have a child and I am expecting another one. Children need security and a safe life. I don't want to have children with unfulfilled needs."

I argued with her and she became angry saying, "If you are such an idealist, why did you marry?"

I said, "You're right. I shouldn't have married."

She said, "I've written to my mother and brother asking them to come and they'll be arriving tomorrow."

That was news for me. I asked why they were coming. She said, "Life with you is not going very well. I would like my mother and brother to talk with you."

I said, "They can't solve any problems which we ourselves can't solve. I don't think it is a very good idea to bring your mother and brother into our problems. We should sort them out ourselves."

She said, "You're so stubborn that I don't think I can get anywhere with you."

This talk left me taken aback, wondering what was happening.

Lata's mother and brother came and we discussed. Lata's mother said "You will never make a good living by writing books. You and Lata's brother should start a drapery shop that will give you a regular income. We will loan you the money."

Although all the male members of my family were successful business men, I couldn't see myself sitting in a shop with a yardstick, measuring cloth to sell and I said so.

Lata's mother went on, "You've had a vagabond life and travelled around the world and now it's time you settled down. I am suggesting this shop because you have no degree or qualifications, so it's the best solution for you."

The three of them were very serious.

Lata said, "You must decide by tomorrow morning what you are going to do. If you don't decide anything positive I cannot stay any longer and shall go with my mother to Bangalore."

Next morning I said, "No, I cannot sit in a shop. I would be a failure. I cannot keep accounts."

Lata's mother said, "Don't worry, my son will take care of the shop. You just sit there."

I said, "No." The discussion ended in argument.

That evening Lata, my daughter, her mother and brother all left together abruptly.

A friend from Delhi, Rajendra, came to see me. He was a novelist. His novels were full of the oppressive atmosphere and taboos of the lower middle-class temperament. He understood very precisely the reasons for the breakdown of my marriage. He was witty and amusing, and a good support for me at that moment. My mother suddenly arrived in Benares, as if she had forgiven my leaving the monkhood. She could not resist her longing to see her son. It was ten years since I had last seen her. It was a happy surprise. She cooked for me and the taste of her simple food was delicious. She had come with expectations of seeing Lata and our baby. Rajendra told her teasingly that I had received a large money award for my adventure, hoping to tempt her to stay with me in Benares. Mother believed that this must be true since for her there was no other explanation of why I had walked round the world. She kept asking about the money and would not accept my word that I hadn't walked for money nor was I given any after the walk. After three weeks I bought her a train ticket home and gave her a little money so that she could go to see the guru, and she left Benares.

One night Rajendra and I took a boat on the Ganges. Rajendra said, "What are you doing after all these fantastic adventures — sitting around moping over your wife and marriage? Come out of this mess. The problem is not how to make your marriage work but to see it as it is and understand it. You have to calm down and leave your mind free and get into something challenging and creative."

We were walking on the other side of the Ganges. The moonlight over the city gave it an eerie silvery glow.

Rajendra said, "Make yourself tough and find your own way. People are going to criticise you whatever you do."

He suggested that I started a Hindi monthly magazine in Delhi to release the ideas and energy which I had gained from going round the world and which couldn't be expressed in getting a conventional job. We talked about the gap between visionaries and activists and about how a magazine could bridge that gap.

We crossed back over the river and, after walking along the ghats, came to the Nepalese temple of Shiva. Shiva the terrible, Shiva the peaceful, Shiva the creator and destroyer, Shiva the symbol of unity, unity in opposites, unity in multiplicity. The god Shiva who drank all the poison of the world which turned his body blue. Shiva who opened a third eye in the centre of his forehead and burnt all the lust and greed of the world with the fire from his eye. In Shiva's presence the breaking of the marriage meant the making of a new life.

I turned to Rajendra and said, "I will come to Delhi and we will start the magazine."

We sat on the steps of the ghat looking at the river flowing by — the Ganges which has been a shelter like a mother for me, a silent witness of everything, never interfering. A body wrapped in yellow cloth was being burnt by the river. I thought of it as myself, the flames burning my marriage. I wanted to find Babaji, but he wasn't there.

I arrived in Delhi. Rajendra met me at the station. I found a flat in Connaught Circus in the centre of Delhi and started working on the magazine, *Vigraha* (Dialectics). After the walk my friends in Calcutta had given me a purse of £2000 and I used this money to start the magazine. The people who want a better society are in two groups. One adopts a liberal-religious approach, with the belief that if you changed each individual everything will be solved. The other believes that if you change the outward conditions, the institutions and environment, the problems will be solved. *Vigraha* was started to bring a synthesis between these two. It presented the heritage of Indian thought which had developed in a village culture and was still preserved there.

One day in the coffee house in Connaught Circus which was the mecca of the Delhi intellectuals, Rajendra introduced me to Dhani, a Marxist from Benares who believed in overthrowing the system by violent means. His ideas challenged my whole thinking about non-violence and I asked him to write a series of articles for *Vigraha*.

Not long after I met Dhani, a violent rebellion broke out in the Naxalbari district in West Bengal organised by the Marxist-Leninist movement. Land had been seized, crops re-distributed, police stations burnt, many landlords killed. The successful revolt in Naxalbari was a challenge to Gramdan and myself. It shook my confidence in non-violence. I felt that the land revolution was turning towards violence. Even Vinoba indicated that the status quo was itself a greater violence than any violent change. It seemed Dhani was right — oppressed people cannot get their minimum rights without checking the greater violence of the oppressors.

After a few days Dhani came to my office with an article on his political ideas. He chain-smoked charminar, a black cigarette. Dhani's serene face and his violent way of expressing his ideas with his hands had hypnotised me. I felt as though he had some power over me. I couldn't sleep, thinking about taking the next train to Naxalbari but I was too weak to take such an action. Instead, to prove to myself that I was still active, I organised a conference on land revolution, during which Gramdan was strongly attacked and criticised by many left-wing writers and politicians. The chairman of Serva Seva Sangh accused me of betraying the non-violent Gramdan movement.

Lata wrote to me that she had given birth to a son but that she was happier without me and would not come back. I went to see her in Bangalore. She said, "I don't think we can be happy together. If you don't want to restrict your freedom and become a family man, how is it possible for us to be together?"

There was a drama going on in Lata's family. Her mother wasn't getting on well with the father who was a sick elderly person, thirty years older than her. The father had left his previous wife and when he married Lata's mother she had been a young village girl of a different caste. The family — Lata, her younger brother and mother — thought that the father had ruined his son's life by not giving him a good education, and his daughter's life by not finding her a good husband. As a result, the family had turned against the father. Lata's mother wanted her to stay at home whereas the father wanted her to go with me. The mother was only interested in me if I could eliminate their dependency on the father. I was only interested in taking Lata and my children away, but Lata wouldn't leave her mother. Our children were in the midst of a conflict between me, Lata and the family. Lata wouldn't let either of the children come with me to Delhi. If we went to court and got divorced, that would bring only a legal solution. I thought that only by letting her do what she wanted could any human solution emerge.

I said to Lata, "The door of my place will always remain open for you."

After a few months Lata came to Delhi and stayed with me, together with the children. I never knew exactly why she came. She arrived with her brother and kept him with her all the time like a shadow.

The atmosphere was tense and we had constant rows over the children. I suggested that one of them could stay with me — my daughter was six and I couldn't see any problems. One day Lata slapped our daughter very hard when she was asking for something. I heard her crying, went to her and took her in my arms. But Lata snatched her away from me saying, "You've nothing to do with the chldren." That made me silent and unresisting, seeing that Lata was ready to use the children as pawns in our conflict. Because I loved my daughter, I wanted to have her with me, and because I loved her I didn't want to fight or be possessive over her. After a month Lata left with the children and I never saw them again.

In Delhi I often went to supper with Rajendra and his wife, Mannu, herself a writer. When I told Mannu how Lata had left me, she jumped from her chair and said, "If she was here I'd kiss her. I'm proud of Lata, walking out on you like that. You men flirting and wandering around and not keeping your relationship fatihfully." Then she turned to Rajendra and said laughingly, "I wish I could do the same."

One night when I was in Delhi I had a dream about Kranti.

Kranti was a very tall white marble statue. The statue was sitting in the lotus position, with a calm, serene and meditative face. I was passing by the statue and suddenly I looked up and recognised Kranti. I put my head on the thigh of the statue and started touching her, "I love you, you are so beautiful, why do you reject me?" The statue started to speak. "What is beautiful in me? My lips — are they beautiful?" She put her hand to her lips and tore them off, "You want my lips to kiss — here they are, kiss them." When she tore her lips off, blood started dripping on me. Then she took her breasts, "You think they're beautiful. You want to touch them?" and gave them to me. Then she gave me her eyes, "You admire my eyes, here they are. Take them if you want to love them." Then she took her hair . . . Suddenly my speech returned. I said, "I don't want your body, I want your soul, you as you are." She said, "If you don't want my body, my soul is always with you, but you have not been satisfied with it." Then she held out both her arms, "I have always loved you but love of body is not real love."

After nine issues of *Vigraha* it became obvious that the magazine wasn't going to be a commercial success. There was too much competition. The £2000 capital with which I had started was used up. I was caught up in financial problems.

It was a hot evening in October. A friend of mine from Benares, Anant, whom I had known for many years, had just come to Delhi for a business deal and was staying with me. We went out to eat, then had some *pan* and bought two cigarettes. It was midnight and Connaught Place was empty. As we walked around, I told Anant about an invitation from Danilo Dolci in Italy to join a walk against the Vietnam war. And Anant was telling me about his profit of £500 from the export of saris.

"I want to go to Italy," I said. "Anant, you've never been out of India. Why don't you come with me? You can bring some samples with you. £500 is just enough to buy two tickets." Anant went back to Benares, consulted his family and sent me a telegram to say that he had bought two plane tickets to London via Rome.

This was a sudden decision. No one knew I was going. I just walked out leaving everything – magazine, office, papers, flat, furniture – to die without me.

Apart from the tickets, Anant and I were only to take out of India £3 each. It was midnight. There was a few moments' panic when the officials took away my papers to check them. But the official returned and everything was in order. I waved goodbye to Kranti and we ran out to the plane. It was a cold November night in 1967, and the journey reminded me of my escape from monkhood.

Floating

Dolci's march from Naples to Rome had already started. We were given a lift to the town where the marchers were staying the night. There were students and young workers, militants of the new left, pacifists and conscientious objectors. Anant and I carried placards and spoke at meetings. We marched to Rome in ten days. There we were joined by a large crowd to demonstrate in front of the American Embassy. After a few days in Rome we flew to Brussels to stay with a friend whom I had met during the walk.

One morning my host read in the papers about an art exhibiton. I was still in bed upstairs, but he shouted up to me because it sounded so exciting. We went to the exhibition. I became enthusiastic about the bold paintings with such primitive colours, and I didn't want to leave without seeing the artist. The paintings communicated to me something fresh and raw. I asked the woman in charge of the gallery if she would give me the artist's address. Instead she promised to pass on my address to the artist.

Next day the artist telephoned and we made an appointment to meet in a coffee bar. The bar was crowded but the moment I entered I saw one person only and that was her. When she talked, her eyes went across my whole body and her hands went in the air, on the table, under the table, all over the place — there was no shyness or inhibition in her at all. Instead of talking about her paintings the first thing she said was, "You are so handsome." That made me shiver. I had never seen any woman so beautiful. I started asking questions, but I didn't know what I was asking nor did I hear what she was answering. We spent three hours in the coffee bar just looking at each other talking.

I said, "You're not a painter, you're a painting."

She laughed and said, "It's good to meet somebody with emotions."

She took me to her house. It was full of paintings and sculptures; and everywhere colours, brushes, stains of spilt paint. Painting for her was not a job but a way of living. The colours were part of her being. Her husband was doing screen printing in the basement. She gave me a present of one of her paintings. It was of a penis, the top of which was very red. On one side was fire and on the other a calm atmosphere of abstract design, the penis being the bridge between opposites.

She kept pouring more wine in my glass.

I said, "I'm not used to drinking so much wine."

She said, "A man coming from the land of the Kama Sutra, Tantra and erotic sculptures must drink wine!"

Later she drove me back. In the car outside she kissed me passionately.

She drove home and immediately telephoned to say that I had left the painting in the back of the car, and asked when I was leaving. Since we were due to fly to London next day, she said she would drive us to the air terminal.

At the terminal we kissed and kissed and she said, "I need more time with you."

While I was in London Marie Clay sent me a painting, together with a letter saying: "My Traveller. You are beautiful, you brought a beautiful moment and a beautiful experience but still unexpressed and longing to be expressed. I dreamt your hair was in my hands and I was holding and moving my fingers through it. After the dream I got up in the night and could not stop myself and took a brush and colours, red and black which you liked most, and painted a picture. I am sending it to you with this letter. For a traveller no destination is far and something tells me you will soon be in Brussels."

In February 1968 we received an invitation to attend a youth conference in Brussels. When we arrived, I telephoned Marie Clay and she came to the house where we were staying.

It was evening and we had dinner with my host. After dinner she whispered in my ear, "Can I stay here tonight?"

I said, "But you're married."

She whispered, "I want you."

She went to the telephone and rang her husband saying straight away, "I'm going to spend the night with Satish."

There was an exchange of heated dialogue on the telephone. Her husband sounded upset and angry.

She said, "I want to have an Indian experience."

Her husband was shouting so loud we could all hear, "Do you think I will lie down in our bed thinking that my wife is in somebody's arms?"

She said, "I don't want to be dishonest with you. We've been married for ten years and I have never gone with anybody else. But

132

tonight I have found someone so attractive that I can't stop myself. Whatever you want to do, you can do, but I'm not coming tonight."

She slammed the receiver down. I was amazed at the passion of her decision.

In the bedroom I kissed her eyes and she kissed my ears, licking them with her tongue. She brought her lips onto my nose and gently bit it, then pressed my head to her breasts, kissing my hair. I opened her shirt and started sucking her nipples, stroking and kissing her warm breasts and belly. She put her hand on my forehead and said, "Relax, let your body rest and feel the touch of my tongue without thinking." There was a complete trust and communication between our two bodies. I lost contact with the outside world totally. My body completely and joyously let go of itself. Marie Clay was a serpent woman, bold and aggressive. In love-making I am more lotus-like – quiet and gentle – therefore there was a perfect union between us. It was the first time I had really experienced the ecstasy in love of a woman and the intensity of sex. Marie Clay gave me full acceptance and feeling of body. I never thought that in the West I would meet someone who was open and who was ready to experience the two bodies meeting in complete sexual fulfillment. The kind of meditation my guru had taught me I felt happening in the complete surrender of two bodies. Through many different postures and positions, I felt my whole body going to a deeper level of consciousness, to a joy where there was total presence of body and soul in the act of making love. Marie Clay released in me the hidden fire.

Next day she telephoned to ask me to have supper with her and her husband.

I was shocked and said, "D'you want your husband to shoot me?"

She explained that she had been completely open and honest with her husband adding, "This is the best part of love. Love knows no guilt. There's nothing to hide."

Marie Clay was a generous friend to me. I could phone up and say "I am here" and she would come. She was an ideal combination of everything I was looking for in Europe. An artist whose life was part of the counter-culture and who in ideas and actions was committed to the radical new left. She was both challenging the taboos and deep-rooted conformism of the old system and living and constructing an alternative life-style among a group of artists in Brussels, Bruges and Ghent. It was as though she wasn't living in a particular place called Brussels, but in herself, and as though she had created a city within a city, a community of free people — painters, poets, playwrights, film-makers and craftsmen. Being with her recharged me. She was like a nest to which I could fly back. I felt a deep communion with her. She wore no mask nor had any pseudo ambitions to be famous or wealthy, but was interested in things as they are. My understanding of India was realised through her. The way she talked and asked questions made me refer back to India.

Marie Clay and I often talked about the new consciousness in Europe. She said "If you want to meet people who are at the centre of alternative living and thinking you must go to Amsterdam.

And so it was. It was the most relaxed city in Europe. It reminded me of Benares — water, small streets and old houses. It was a city where life was integrated. I met small groups of young people finding a peaceful corner to live, starting their own communities and expressing themselves through crafts, art and music. In their way of living there was a simple human relationship and love, a softness, an openness, an emptiness which allowed others to penetrate into their hearts. The homes, sometimes boats, where they lived were very different. They had few possessions and mostly made by hand, and there was beautiful music. They made their own bread and co-operated with other communities, selling their things between themselves, doing yoga and meditation and pursuing an inner life, creating an island of their own beautiful utopia. They were spreading their ideas by communicating on a very personal level. The Europe of science and technology seemed far removed from the warm vibrations and love in their company. There was a quietness on their faces, and in that quietness a deep smile, a selfless smile, a smile without any expectation, without any desire, just receiving. They didn't tell me how they wanted to put the world in order. They were not interested in my philosophy. I could sit down, rest and be quiet. This way I could be in touch with the hearts of people and not just with their minds.

Anant and I travelled by train to Paris, Geneva, Zurich, Vienna and Belgrade. We carried rucksacks, a change of clothes, a blanket and toothbrush. I felt a beautiful emptiness inside me. I had forgotten all the problems that had troubled me in India. I was floating with the wind, and wherever the wind took me I went. I was meeting people, eating and dancing with them, seeing rivers, coming across new cities and countries. If I met somebody and he said, "Come here", I would go. And whenever there was a meeting, I would put out my handkerchief for people to pay my travel expenses to the next city or country.

In Belgrade Anant and I were staying in a youth hostel. We met someone who was driving from Belgrade to Stockholm and then back to Istanbul. He offered us a lift. I did not want to drive so fast through Europe. But Anant decided to take the lift to see Scandinavia before returning to India from Istanbul. After travelling together for five months, we parted. Then I travelled to Budapest, Prague, Berlin and London.

The Soviet Government had given me an Award for my book *Around the World without a Penny* and a certificate for 'outstanding work for peace and freedom'. I went to the Soviet Embassy in London and was received by the cultural attache. I asked him what was the point in giving awards to foreign writers and putting Soviet writers in prison. I wanted to return my award but he refused to take it. I came out of the Embassy, tore it up in the street and threw it into a dustbin. I sent the money back.

I came once more to Belgium and spent two weeks in the seaside town of Knokke. Late one night I received a phone call from War Resisters International in London. Czechoslovakia had been invaded by the members of the Warsaw pact and War Resisters asked me if I would go to Budapest to join a small group to protest against the invasion. Similar groups were to be sent to Moscow, Warsaw and Berlin.

I went to Brussels and applied for a visa but was told that because I had 'journalist' written in my passport, application had to be approved by the foreign ministry in Budapest.

After a week of nothing happening, I left for Vienna. There I got the same answer. In the Embassy I saw an advertisement for Malev, the Hungarian airline, together with a note on an arrangement for getting visas at the airport in Budapest. I bought an air ticket and arrived at the Budapest airport.

When the authorities saw my passport, they said "You're a journalist. You can't come in like this."

"Now I'm here" I answered.

Rejecting the *Peace Prize*

It was Sunday. They said I had to report to the foreign ministry the following day and gave me a visa for twenty-four hours. The next day I got a four-day visa from the foreign ministry. I met the four other members of the protest group in a cafe. One of them was Wolfgang who had been in jail with me in Paris in 1963. They had got through customs with leaflets in German and Hungarian strapped to their bodies. We planned the demonstration.

On 24 September 1968 in Liberation Square we put up a large banner – END THE OCCUPATION OF CZECHOSLOVAKIA. A nearby policeman paid no attention until we started handing out leaflets to a large crowd which soon gathered. Ten minutes later the banner was torn down by plainclothes' policemen. The crowd was broken up and the five of us arrested and taken to a barber's snop until a police van arrived. We were told that giving our subversive leaflets in a socialist country meant from six months to three years in prison. That night we were driven to the political police headquarters then to a large fortress which was a prison. They put us in separate cells and gave us prisoner's uniforms.

In the interrogations which followed the authorities wanted to know why we had chosen Budapest, what was behind our demonstration, who financed it and who was our leader. After three days of hard interrogation, we were all expelled and driven to the Austrian border.

When last I was in Budapest I had met a Hungarian painter, Hinsz Gyula, who gave me a painting on the theme of African liberation. It was a large painting and a rucksack wanderer of my kind would be unable to carry it and keep it safely. Nevertheless it was so beautiful and precious that I took it with me to Prague. At breakfast in the hotel I sat with Canon John Collins who was attending a peace conference. Canon Collins is a champion of African liberation. It is not only the present which is important but it must be given to the right recipient. Canon Collins I realised was the '*supatra*' (the right pot) for the gift. I gave him the painting. He invited me to Britain to give a series of lectures on the Gandhian approach to peace, sponsored by Christian Action. I had accepted. So now I went to England for a month's lecture tour.

Afterwards I travelled to Germany and met some German friends who were going to India in a Mini-bus. We planned to travel together. Two days before we were due to leave, Canon Collins telephoned me from London. He said he was receiving enthusiastic reports of my lecture tour and wanted me to follow up with a further six months' lecturing in London. I myself had been impressed by the interest shown by people during my tour — it seemed that the time was ripe for these ideas. So I wrote letters to people I knew all over India to ensure that my German friends would be received as if I was with them and then went back to London.

Two months later, with the help of Canon Collins, I started the London School of Non-Violence, and my book *Non-Violence or Non-Existence,* was published to coincide with the opening of the school.

In London I lived a static life. I was no longer a wanderer. The city with its pressures, travelling in the underground, living in the crowds, shopping centres, fumes and the whole consumer world was getting in my head and in my nose. I got the feeling that some part of me was dying, some part of me was suppressed. My legs were itching to be on the road and my eyes to see the blue sky over trees and mountains and rivers and deserts.

Canon Collins had promised to pay my plane fare back to India, but I persuaded him to buy me a second-hand car instead. It was Gandhi's centenary year. I painted a map of my overland route to India on the car together with several quotations from Gandhi, wrote to various people and groups on the way, then set out from London with two others.

In France and Italy we stayed in various communities, talking about non-violence to small groups. In Eastern Europe and the Middle East we usually slept out by the road. Sometimes we stayed in Indian Embassies. For several days in Syria we stayed with a Palestinian leader and argued the issues of non-violence with him. In Damascus we rested a few days and smoked houkas and hashish, then drove across the desert to Baghdad.

In Teheran I received permission to be in Pakistan for seven days. I was the first Indian allowed to pass through since the 1965 war between India and Pakistan.

We reached the borders of Pakistan at the Khyber Pass in the evening. Next day a jeep arrived with several plainclothes policemen to escort us through Pakistan. In Rawalpindi we went to the chairman of the Rotary Club who had given me a great welcome when I had been walking. When I asked him for hospitality, he reminded me of the 1965 war and said he dared not give us hospitality because people would say he was siding with the Indians. We tried some hotels, but it was the same story. Finally after two hours' driving around the town, we found a small hotel which was willing to put us up.

Fifteen minutes after we arrived, several hundred people had gathered round the car in the street outside the hotel shouting "Where is the messenger of Gandhi? Take this message to India — we don't need Gandhi, we don't need Indians here."

They were shouting to burn the car. We ran out of the hotel. People started hitting us and shouting "Kill them, shoot them." We jumped into the car, started it and drove through the crowd. The jeep with the plainclothes policemen was nowhere in sight. A tyre had been let down. We found a quite street, changed the tyre and drove to the Indian High Commission in Islamabad. Next day we drove non-stop through Pakistan to the Indian border.

Mukti

After driving eighty days we arrived in Delhi on 2 October 1969, Gandhi's centenary day. Posters lined the streets. Near Gandhi's grave a gigantic twenty-million rupee exhibition had been set up, showing his life and message.

I went to Rajgir where Vinoba had organised a Gramdan conference. Rajgir is surrounded by five hills from which hot springs of healing water flow. On the peaks of these hills Mahavir lived his ascetic life. Here Buddha preached his sermons. Here also many Hindu rishis taught *The Upanishads*.

Tens of thousands of people were gathered, everybody living in tents. Buddhist monks in their saffron robes had come from many countries to attend the conference. Many friends of mine were also there.

On the last day of the conference Vinoba, who was seventy-four, declared that he was retiring and would return to his ashram in Pawnar. He said that although he was willing to give advice and answer letters, he was too old and ill to continue to be active.

When Vinoba left for Pawnar I went to Benares. I searched for Dhani knowing that he was involved in the underground Naxalite movement. It was a tense time for the Naxalites. Since I had been away, the Naxalite movement had become strong in Bihar and Bengal, especially in Calcutta where Naxalite activity had created such panic that it was virtually a police state. Every day there were bombings, killing of landlords and police.

After telephoning friends who might know Dhani's whereabouts, I was given an address. I went to the house. I was told he had left a few days before, but the people there gave me another address. He had also left that place. Every address I went to, it was the same story. Dhani was in hiding, changing his address to prevent anyone from finding him. I left messages at the various addresses, asking him to contact me.

Late one night when everyone else was asleep and it was totally quiet, I was woken by a knock at the door. It was Dhani. "All those who want real revolution should join this movement" Dhani said.

His eyes penetrated into me. The power of his argument was less strong than the power of his eyes and his physical presence, especially late at night in the small dark room with only a lantern burning.

Dhani said "The establishment and the landlords will never give up unless there is an armed struggle. The enemy today is subtle and difficult to pin down. We cannot use the same tactics and strategy as Gandhi used during the independence movement."

I said "The state is too powerful for armed resistance. We have to find another way."

We smoked and talked all night.

"The time isn't ripe for an armed revolution." I said.

Dhani replied "The time will never be right if we sit quiet."

I said "Unless the oppressed are aware of their oppression, they will never get rid of it."

"Our task is to fight on their behalf" he said.

When the light started to come, he said he couldn't stay any more – it was dangerous for him to be in the streets in daylight.

He left and I lay down but couldn't sleep. My mind was spinning round and round.

After the Rajgir conference Vinoba had designated one of his closest disciples, Krishna Raj Bhai, together with about a hundred Gramdan workers, to carry out the actual implementation of Gramdan into reality in Saharsa district. Saharsa is one of the poorest parts of Bihar – where 70 per cent of the people were landless labourers. Krishna Raj Bhai was a close friend of mine. He wrote to me:

"If Gramdan succeeds in Saharsa, the movement succeeds for the whole of India. The Naxalite movement is spreading into Saharsa and has made people believe that unless there is an armed struggle nothing is going to change. This is the testing point, the last battle for victory. I would like you to come here." So I went to Saharsa.

The town of Saharsa was neither a village nor a city. It was a newly created government settlement with badly built houses and shacks, crowded with the landless from the villages and the jobless from the city. There were over 500 villages in Saharsa district which was divided into 22 blocks, each block having its headquarter town under which there were a number of villages. A hundred Gramdan workers were divided up amongst the 22 blocks, with Krishna Raj Bhai acting as co-ordinator. I was assigned the task of organising land distribution in the village of Chattupur.

As I was walking to Chattapur along a car track, a man suddenly stepped out of a bamboo thicket onto the path. He was dressed in labourer's clothes and carried a long, oiled bamboo stave, *lathi*.

"Where are you going?" he demanded aggressively.

"What's it to you where I'm going?" I replied.

"What are you here for, then?"

"I'm a Gramdan worker," I replied.

"Keep off this area and don't come to interfere and delay our revolution. You might distribute some land, which is probably barren since the landlord didn't want it, and you'll make a big noise about it. What is a little bit of land? Hardly enough for a dozen families. Let the dissatisfaction get deeper into the hearts of people and let the landless, who are in the majority, unite together to fight the landlords. Only then will this problem be solved."

I asked him how he thought the revolution would take place.

"Revolution will come when every peasant rises up and seizes all the land, every inch of it." His voice was strong and full of conviction. "Vinoba is a saint perhaps, but a state-appointed saint. He never says anything against the government."

I asked, "Are you a Naxalite?"

"There's no such thing as Naxalism," he replied impatiently. "That's just a name given by the press. We are Marxist-Leninists."

After that he remained silent and at the next village turned to go.

Chattapur was a large village. The rich lived in the wide square bazaar in large brick houses, replacing the thatched roofs with 'modern' corrugated iron. In the front courtyards stood large granaries, the symbol of wealth. The labourers lived in ghettos in the surrounding neighbourhood, so overcrowded that the little bamboo huts stood back to back, each family sprawling into the next. I was invited to stay at the local school. That evening I went to an area where the landless labourers lived. Men sat round the glow of a straw fire, I greeted them, but their reply was silence and suspicious glances. I edged my way into the circle and introduced myself.

"Chattapur is a Gramdan village, isn't it?' I asked.

They replied, "The Vinoba people came a long time ago and took signatures – they promised us land. Then some communists came and promised to give land. And the government official has been promising for the last year. But it seems as if we won't get anything until after we are dead. At the moment we're not even sure if our huts are safe, and our masters have given notice to stop us share-cropping their land."

A young voice spoke out of the darkness. "A few days ago a strange man came here. He said he was a new kind of communist and that the old communists who came before had made a pact with the landlords and they won't help us any more. He said that voting is no more use now and we will have to fight the landlords ourselves, and that in some districts the fighting has already begun. We might have to kill our masters, he said, because unless we do something and are ready to act ourselves, we will never get land. Is that true?"

"Was he from Chattapur?" I asked.

"He came from outside. He didn't tell us his name. He just arrived one evening, bringing his food. He stayed for two or three hours and left the same night. He belonged to our caste though."

How could I hope to win their support and gain their confidence by giving more words, then deserting them again? What right had I to try to create a suspicion in their minds against a man who came from the same caste, brought his food and experienced the exploitation, not merely intellectually but physically? After all what was I? Someone who wore clothes worth enough to feed a whole family for a month. What a vast gulf separated them from me. Why should they believe me? Dozens of politicians and Gramdan workers had come before, and what could I tell them that was new?

I said, "When the time comes to kill the landlord, we'll see. But at the moment why don't we try to get the land some other way first? If you're all ready we can ask the landlord straight out. If it works, why resort to violence?"

Heads nodded slowly in agreement, but not confidently. They could only see the landlords in their normal role — oppressors who goaded them to work harder and harder. I was seized by a feeling of frustration as I gazed into the leaping flames, watching the straw consumed to white-hot ashes. The heat was scorching and the density of human suffering enclosed us within their glowing circle.

After seeing the despair and hopelessness of the landless and the cynical resistence of the landlords in Chattapur I wrote to Vinoba. He asked me to come and see him. So I went. I stood in the open temple. The sun on the marble floor felt hot under my feet. I walked across the floor and settled down into a cool quiet corner. For a long time there was no sound. The only movement was from a thin strand of smoke, emerging from burning incense, which curled and billowed and faded into nothing. The bright orange flowerheads shone against the rough dark stone. A murmur of voices drew nearer. Then slowly in threes and fours, people gathered for prayers. Their clothes were crumpled and drab, made from various shades of *khadi* (homespun cotton) and different styles. One or two women had shaven heads and wore the saffron robes of *sanyasinis* (ascetics). They sat together in small groups, talking in low voices and whispers. Suddenly a hush fell over the temple. Vinoba, dressed in his short loincloth, walked slowly towards us, surrounded by his attendants, friends and disciples. He wore his green cap with the peak pulled down over his eyes. He sat down in the centre of the floor and we all joined together in prayer.

Next day I went to talk to him. He took off his watch and placed it on the little desk in front of him, reached for his glasses and put them on his nose. Suddenly he started shining as though he had switched himself on like a light bulb. Light was there, illuminating everything.

He said, "All these confusions come because we are living in the mind. We have concepts, conclusions and expectations before we act. Therefore our action is not pure action. We have to lift ourselves above the ego mind. There are two important things in life – the Ultimate and the Intimate. The Intimate is important because you must be involved with the things which directly affect you and the people around you. The Ultimate is important because it is something far away. It is like a pole star to guide and give direction to your life. You do not have to reach your Ultimate, because it's not a thing to be achieved. Life is the line between the Intimate and Ultimate, between the near and the far. As you experience life, you will be part of the process between the farthest point and the nearest. It is the line which is important to experience, not 'getting' anywhere.

"King Janak was a supreme example of the unity between the Intimate and Ultimate. He did not leave the Intimate in order to achieve the Ultimate. He fulfilled his activities as a king with a detached mind and still soul. One day god Vishnu praised this king in front of all the gods. One of the gods of evil spirit cast doubts on the king's detachment, saying to Vishnu, "He's a king and can afford to be detached. If you allow me to test him, I can prove that this detachment is a facade."

Vishnu allowed him to go to test the king. The god of evil spirit chose a day when the king was resting in one of his palaces in the outskirts of his city and came in the form of a Brahmin priest. By his power he created in front of the king a scene of the whole capital under fire – his army quarters, his palace, the market place and houses. The Brahmin said, "Our city is burning to ashes. O King, you must do something to save it." The king said, "In this burning city nothing burns of mine."

I stayed in the ashram for a few days more. I saw Vinoba often – at his manual labour, his prayers or talking to his old friend with whom he played chess. Being with Vinoba for me was like having a bathe in the Ganges. I felt relaxed. Whenever I went to him, I found light. He had never given me any solution in words nor did he try to show me the path. Without him saying too much, I could understand. It was a vibration, a feeling. I realised that my disappointment with the movement was with myself. Basically I had been looking to the movement for the fulfillment of my own ambitions and desires to confront and to win. Therefore by being critical of the movement, I had merely been expressing my own weaknesses and unfulfilled ambitions. When I was young I learnt the philosophy of Completeness. It is summed up in *The Upanishads* – "This is complete, that is complete. Whatever comes to us from the complete and whatever has emerged out of the complete is complete. If you take something from the complete, what remains is still complete." When I looked closely at my life, I realised this sense of completeness was only a theory for me. A deep cry came – how could I make myself a complete being?

In the years after the walk I had given hundreds of speeches, written articles, books and letters. But I was unable to find self-fulfillment. I was caught up in illusions of change, all the time talking about 'revolution'. I had a mask on my face and I was living in the illusion that the mask was a reality. Caught in duality, I was searching for my soul.

One night in Benares after hours in bed tossing from one side to the other, I got up, had a bath and phoned Anant. "Can I come to see you or can you come here?" I said. Anant said he would come in the evening. I said "I can't wait till evening. You must come now. I have something I want to talk to you about."

He came to see me. We had breakfast together and talked.

I said "I have been living too long in cities and artificial gardens. I am ready to get out and find a place to think and experiment, where I can find my own way."

He said "My father has a farm. It's a place in the forest with very few people. I would also like to leave Benares and could persuade my father to give us some land."

I said "Can we go tomorrow to see the place?"

Next morning at dawn we drove out of Benares then headed south in the Vindhaya mountains.

We arrived at Jumudi village where Anant's father had his farm, got out of the car and sat under a mango tree by a well. Some villagers brought us a pomegranite, papaya and other fruit. The village consisted of tribal mud huts, with coloured clay painted on the walls. Around the huts were the animals − goats, cows and buffalos. There was a large monsoon pond with buffalos floating in it.

We walked into the forest to see the land. The forest was silent and full of herb and fruit trees, and there was a river. This was the right place for me. I built my own little hut and started living among the tribal people. I worked on the land, grew vegetables, and cooked food.

Gradually more people came and we made a community which we called 'Nidam', meaning 'The Nest'. We had twenty-five acres of land which Anant's father gave us as a gift, and we each had our own hut built with mud, wood and a thatched roof of straw. We grew our own food and had our own milk.

There was no water on the land. We asked a man from the village to help us locate water. He walked around looking at the colour of the leaves and vegetation, then told us to begin digging near some anthills.

For three months we dug with pickaxes and spades, our bodies covered with earth from lifting it and carrying it in buckets on our heads. We went on digging, trying to finish it by the beginning of the monsoon. When we had dug thirty feet deep, we hit rock. We went on digging. One day the earth started bubbling. We had hit the water.

The monsoon was over and everyone was busy harvesting. Every day was spent out in the fields with the people, cutting the golden brown rice with a sickle and stacking it in rows. The whole village co-operated. One day people gathered to harvest one farmer's land, then they moved on to harvest another's. When all the grain was gathered in, the farmers distributed it to the craftsmen of the villages — shoemaker, carpenter, potter, washerman, cowherd, blacksmith and the brahmin priest — to settle accounts until the next harvest came. Then there was a big festival to mark the completion of the harvest — *diwali*, the festival of lights. The people ate, drank, dressed up and danced and went around from village to village.

Every morning I got up with the sunrise. After doing yoga and working in the fields, I lay down under the sun and was massaged by other community members, feeling the slow touch and quiet movement of hands on the body, feeling the muscles and nerves and bones and flesh relaxing to the maximum. Then I sat down and with mustard oil I massaged each toe of my foot and each part of the ankles and heels and instep. Afterwards I bathed at the well.

Gardening became a real joy — looking at each plant growing every day then seeing leaves coming then flowers and after a few days the fruit becoming bigger and bigger, and every day weeding, putting water and manure and tying plants with string if they fell down.

Some days I walked by myself in the river bed which had many bends. There were trees with roots exposed by the river, and flowers and the leaves and butterflies all around. Other days I went with the village people to get honey from the forest trees, they made a fire under a tree and waited until the honey dripped into a pot under the combs.

Every night the tribal people lit a bonfire. A lot of people gathered round it. Someone started playing the flute and drums and all the tribal people joined in, singing and dancing and chanting, going deeper into the night, deeper into the music, deeper into the flames of the fire. In their chanting and dancing and music, they forgot everything and became absolutely absorbed in it, in union with themselves and the whole existence. I found a world where there was integrated life and where I could journey inwards and bring my mind to rest. I found a balance between the positive and negative. I saw unity, I saw the harmony between the inner and outer, I saw the opposites as one. Life was relaxed. It didn't matter what direction the life took or even if there was a direction or not.

One morning I got up early and walked into the forest. It was dawn. There was dew on the grass and leaves. I came to a tall tree with large overhanging branches, sat down cross-legged under the tree and closed my eyes. I looked into my body and saw a dark tunnel, a deep hollow inside. I went into it, drawn inwards.

Instead of smelling outside, my nose was smelling the inner happenings and my ears were hearing the sounds inside. I could hear the sounds and voices of the ego pushing me in different directions. But I sat quietly. Slowly the battle calmed down, it slowly faded away. Gradually peace came.

I saw the events of my life as one thread, the same thread which united the whole universe and which was each person. I saw a struggle without conflict, a pain without misery. I saw a love so great that it had to remain hidden. I felt myself part of my mother and father, and in all the people through whom I had been expressed. I was being reborn. I felt like a child, like an innocent person, just living and growing, engaged in the journey from action to non-action, from struggle without to struggle within, a journey to the centre, the source, searching for the lost self, the soul.

Everything became meditation. I felt a sense of divinity. This newness brought a surrender, a surrender where nothing mattered, where everything was accepted. It was beyond happiness, beyond pleasure. I experienced the zero level of existence, the void, the beauty of the void and the beauty of zero, the beauty of nothingness.

I opened my eyes. I saw a snake about three yards long curled round the trunk of the tree beside me. I sat still. The snake disappeared into a hole among the roots.

I must have sat there for six hours because when I returned it was after ten o'clock.

One morning after I had been in the forest for a year, I walked with Anant to the town of Anupur, five miles away, to buy some food in the market that was held there every Wednesday.

There was an astrologer in the market place who predicted the future by calculating how the stars and planets affected a person at a particular moment. He was a coarse-faced *sadhu*, skinny and dark, with a shaven head and light brown robe, sitting on the floor cross-legged with a young disciple and several townspeople sitting around. When I arrived he opened his eyes then asked me why I had come so late? The way he spoke, it was as if he had been waiting for me. I didn't answer.

He said, "I speak only between nine and twelve o'clock, and after twelve I keep silent. Now it's coming close to twelve."

He went on "You have a very good friend. He trusts you, you trust him. He supports you in everything. You are happy with his support. But his wife thinks you are an enemy. She wants to change her husband's mind. She quarrels with him and with you"

That was my relationship with Anant and his wife.

The astrologer said "He is giving you land, but there are some difficulties in getting the land transferred in the name of the community."

It was true.

Then he said "Very soon you are going on a long journey beyond the ocean . . ."

I interrupted him, saying that I had just returned from a long journey and had no desire to go away again.

"What I see, I tell you" he said. "Once you are in the far land, you are going to travel by car and you are going to meet someone in that land who will completely change your life."

He paused then said "Now it's twelve o'clock. It's time for my silence and I cannot speak anymore. If you want to contact me or ask any more questions, this is my address."

He gave his name and address near Delhi, then closed his eyes and withdrew into himself. I gave him a gift of five rupees and left.

The war began in Bangladesh and millions of refugees started pouring into India.

I left the community to work in the refugee camps. While I was there, Canon Collins wrote asking me to give him a first-hand account of what was happening, then suggested I come to England with information and photographs to put on an exhibition about Bangladesh which Christian Action would sponsor.

I collected photographs of the refugees and the liberation army and flew to London.

The exhibition was held in London in July 1971. I asked Operation Omega* for someone to talk at the exhibition. They sent June.

As soon as she walked into the room, my whole attention was drawn towards her. She was quiet and serene, and when she talked she

* Formed to get peace workers across the borders into Bangladesh

spoke with precise words.

After the meeting I said to her "I'm planning to take this exhibition around Europe. Would you like to come to speak about Bangladesh?"

She said "No".

Operation Omega gave me £40 towards travelling in Europe and someone drove me to Amsterdam, Sweden, Denmark and Germany. From Germany I went by train to Austria, Switzerland, France, then Italy — holding press conferences, meetings and lectures wherever I went. I was in Rome in December staying with the abbot of San Paolo monastery when the news of the independence of Bangladesh reached me.

On Christmas Eve I had a dream.

I was looking for someone and I found him. It was Keval who used to lead us when I was a Jain monk. I asked him to show me the way to my destination. On the way we passed through a village. Keval's wife was sitting outside his house. She wanted him to stay at home because he had been away for a long time. Keval pointed out the direction to me, saying he would catch up after spending a few moments with his wife. He went into the house and I continuéd. After climbing over a sandhill, I found myself in the city of Allahabad where there is a confluence of the three holy rivers — the Ganges, Yamuna and Saraswati. There were uncountable numbers of pilgrims — naked monks, Hindu sanyasis, Buddhists, Jain monks, religious brahmins — all bathing in the river, thousands of women in saris in many colours. Green dust was spread over everywhere. By the side of the rivers were some huts in which there were astrologers and palmists. I went into one of the huts and sat by an astrologer, waiting for Keval. The astrologer asked to see my palm. I gave him my palm. He started speaking to me in French, telling me I was going to reach my destination. Suddenly I saw a girl I knew. She was naked and resting her breasts on the astrologer's head, laughing at me. I turned away and looked towards the rivers outside the hut. From the confluence of the three rivers I saw a man emerging and becoming bigger and bigger and bigger. He went on growing till he became like a pillar between the earth and the sky. He was naked — his head, arms, legs, penis, stomach, chest, everything was huge. As I watched, he started to become smaller and walked towards me. He came nearer and he was wearing clothes. He was a normal-sized man. I left the hut and went back to look for Keval.

When I reached his house I found him asleep. I left him and continued walking. After a while I found myself in a temple in a halo of lights with many colours. In this temple I saw Keval and my guru, the girl and the astrologer, and also the man who had stood as a pillar between the sky and the earth. Everybody was there, and they were all celebrating. Everyone was full of joy.

After Christmas I came to London where I received the news of my mother's death.

"At the age of eighty your mother had felt that she had served the family and had fulfilled all her duties and that now it was time for her to meet death. She decided to separate herself from her worn-out body by fasting. She had no fear of death. She believed that only death could bring new life and that she must die to live again. She went round the town, to family and friends, saying goodbye and asking forgiveness for any wrong she had done. The next day at sunrise she took no more food or drink except a little boiled water. The news of your mother's fast unto death spread by word of mouth. Monks came to bless her and be blessed since it was considered a brave and holy way of dying – to embrace death rather than letting it capture you unaware. Hundreds of people came to have her last *darshan* and to ask for forgiveness. She didn't talk much but by her look acknowledged the receiving and giving of forgiveness. People sat outside singing hymns and praying. After thirty-five days of fasting your mother died."

One day in February I went to an Operation Omega meeting where I met June again. A few days later I went to watch her making pottery. Afterwards we had a cup of tea.

I said to her "Tell me something about yourself."

She talked about her relationships. We spent the evening together in a pub.

For three weeks after that I heard nothing from her. I phoned her at work and was told she was ill.

I went to see her at her home. I knocked on the door. For a few minutes nothing happened. Then she opened the door. She was in her dressing-gown.

I stepped back and said "How are you? I hear you're not well."

She smiled and said "Come in."

I came in and she shut the door.

June was alone in the house and she had not eaten all day. I went to the kitchen and found half a cabbage. I put the cabbage soup on to boil then took some oil from the kitchen and massaged June's stomach, head, legs and feet. Later I gave her the soup to drink. I read to her and she fell asleep. As she was sleeping, I looked closely at her face, wondering if this was the person the astrologer in India had said would change my life. That night I slept downstairs on a couch and next morning got up early to make some tea. June got well soon and her home became my home. Spring came and we sat in the garden. Memories and contacts with India, family and friends seemed like a thousand years ago. My beard and hair grew long with love.

June told me of a dream she often used to have in her childhood. A vast desert stretched out before her and in the distance was a figure. It was a man walking across the desert towards her. She was terrified. She always woke up before the man could reach her, while he was still walking, never reaching his destination.

In the summer we travelled from London to Stockholm to attend a conference and stayed for two weeks in the flat of a leather-craftsman. The flat was peaceful and smelled sweetly of leather. There, feeling the doubtlessness of our relationship, feeling a sense of warmth, touch and belonging, we conceived a child.

In the autumn we went to live in a commune of European peace workers in a small village in Germany. There June and I worked in the garden, cooked together, did yoga and meditation, and every afternoon for an hour went walking together — sometimes to the forest near the house, sometimes along a river called 'the inner stream', sometimes to the town three miles away. We enjoyed the trees and air and fields and told each other stories. Then every evening I massaged June with oil and felt the child move as I was massaging her stomach.

We thought that what we were feeling should be the name of our child. We decided to use the name 'Mukti' which means 'freedom' in Sanskrit.

At the beginning of March 1973, just before Mukti was due, we returned to London by train.

I had a dream.

I woke up June, saying "I know where my soul is. Hurry let's go." We started walking and came to a thick dark forest. June held onto my

Satish and June

shirt. Then we climbed mountains so high we passed through the clouds. Coming down the other side, we were stopped by soldiers who allowed us to cross their country only if we did it in one day and didn't stay the night. They escorted us. Suddenly other soldiers started shooting at us. We came to a river. June and I walked on opposite banks. I became a woman in a pink and orange dress. A man rode towards us on an elephant, peered closely at us then rode on. June walked over the water to me and we shouted to the man on the elephant. He told us he was searching for Satish to tell him not to worry, his soul was safe. I said I was Satish. He was surprised I was woman. He turned his elephant round and rode in front of us. Another man rode up on horseback. The man said they were following him. I saw mountains in the distance. Night fell. I saw a long line of people coming down the mountain-side with flaming torches, disappearing and appearing again as they came down a winding path. We walked on. The procession came towards me, one of the people carrying a golden box on his head. I opened it. Inside was a bundle of silk cloth which I unwrapped. Inside the silk was a lotus and wrapped in the petals of the lotus I found the word '*Atman*'. I had found my soul.

A few days later Mukti was born. I sat on the bed beside June, helping her to push. In a moment of birth I was holding June's body in my arms, June was pushing and Mukti was revealed.

I can't imagine what life would have been for me without the canal leading from Camden to Regents Park. From spring to summer I would rise early and take a walk along the canal and run barefoot on the cool grass of the park. Squeaking squirrels, tall trees, and the quacking ducks swimming in the lakes, this was the oasis of green peace surrounded by the automobile traffic jams vomiting fumes and like a tunnel the canal leads to this oasis hardly noticing the monstrosity of industrial London.

When I missed my morning yoga of the walk, I would go with Mukti and June in the afternoon. One such afternoon returning to Kentish Town, I saw a man busy planting out flowers in a window box. He resembled John Papworth, but it couldn't be, since he was in Zambia working as an advisor to President Kaunda and if he should be in London he would surely be in his own comfortable house in St. John's Wood. As I was discounting the fact, he turned and I saw that truly it was John Papworth. We fell into each other's arms filled with the pleasure of meeting. He invited us in. Almost the first thing he said was that *Resurgence* magazine which he had founded was about to be closed down for the want of an editor, an editor who would work for love. "So Satish, God sent me to find you here and I dare say that you will be the editor and let us speak no more." I was taken aback. "I have never learnt English, had no schooling and I can't spell a word. True, I can read and speak, but with this little knowledge of English, how can I edit a magazine of *Resurgence's* Repute?"

"Yes you can and you will, especially with the help of your companion, June, you will have no trouble." Thus fell Resurgence in my lap. It was summer 1973. I decided to put my energies into Resurgence for a year or so and get it off the ground once again. I didn't like to deny the request of an old friend or to refuse something which was coming to me as of fate. I decided to put off thoughts of returning to India with June and Mukti until the end of 1975.

I should have known that life does not operate on the basis of plans, no matter how rational. My nature is to let things happen rather than make them happen and I should stick to it. So the plan to go to India was interrupted by the onset of dictatorial rule there in June 1975. A large number of my friends and colleagues were put behind bars. A total censorship of the press and curtailment of normal civil liberties was enforced. Most of all the arrest of J. P. Narayan with whom I had worked closely was the greatest shock.

I cancelled the scheduled meeting of the London School of Non-Violence and instead held an emergency meeting on India. Nearly 100 people gathered at the school in the crypt of St. Martin in the Fields. From there we launched the *Free JP campaign* and invited Philip Noel-Baker, who in the British Parliament had moved the Bill for the Independence of India, to preside over it. Some of the other active members were Paul Connett, Dharampal Sarur Hoda and Hans Janicek. I edited and produced a fortnightly newsheet 'Swaraj', a digest of news and comment about India published in the European and American papers. This circulated clandestinely in India from hand to hand and was even smuggled into prisons. This voice of solidarity strengthened the courage and the struggle of the resistance movement. My own return to India was postponed indefinitely since there was no point in walking into a jail, which my friends in India wrote would be my fate. I could perhaps help the resistance movement more from the outside. Sarur and others had their passports impounded and my name was certainly on the government's list.

I organised the first European Sarvodaya conference in the Conway Hall to introduce the true nature of J.P.'s people movement as well as to show the relevance of Gandhi's ideas to western industrial societies, Lanza del Vasto, E. F. Schumacher, John Seymour, Leopold Kohr, Edward Goldsmith, and Thich Nhat Hanh were among the speakers. Five hundred people attended.

The conference made me think that as I was not returning to India I should find a place in a rural area, where I could combine the intellectual work of editing *Resurgence* with the manual work of growing food. Editing and publishing *Resurgence*, a magazine advocating decentralisation, from the megapolitan centre of London, was not in keeping with our aims so when the opportunity presented itself of moving to Wales, I welcomed it. Wales is a small nation, it has not lost its cultural identity and I feel here so much at home, it is another India for me. The hills of the Prescelis and the gentler slopes of Carn Ingli have arrested my heart. When I came to live here, I made a vow that I would not travel out of Wales for one year and I would allow myself to take root and learn the Welsh language.

Being here on the farm I can live a life in tune with nature and the seasons. Milking the cow, splitting wood, sitting by a log fire are the true pleasures of life here. My needs are very small. I need no restaurant, no theatre, no cinema, no television, no car. I can scarcely spend on myself more than £5 a week. This reduction on the external expanded life has increased the expansion within. I am closer to Jain practice here than for many years, the Mantra of Surrender comes to me much more easily than ever before. The longer I am away from India the more I take sustenance from my roots in India. Although my habits, my manners and my language become more western, within myself I discover more and more an India which is beyond nation and geography. I am living two Ashrams simultaneously. My responsibility for the household is intermingled with dedication to the community at large. And I dream of relinquishing my household responsibility at the age of fifty and submerging myself totally in the third stage of life — action without any reward or responsibility, leading towards a freedom from all commitments so that I can die with pleasure as much as I have lived with pleasure.

Cancelled from
Gladstone's Library

2 4 JUL 2024

GLADSTONE'S
LIBRARY

ST DEINIOL'S LIBRARY
HAWARDEN